A CASE OF LIBEL

A Case

A Play in Three Acts

 Random House • New York

# of Libel

by HENRY DENKER

Based on the book
My Life in Court by Louis Nizer

8/2
D

A CASE OF LIBEL *was first presented by Roger L. Stevens and Joel Schenker at the Longacre Theatre, New York City, on October 10, 1963, with the following cast:*

(IN ORDER OF APPEARANCE)

CLAIRE MARSHALL	Camila Ashland
ABNER COLES	Joseph Julian
DAVID STRONG	Joel Crothers
ROBERT SLOANE	Van Heflin
DENNIS CORCORAN	John Randolph
ANITA CORCORAN	M'el Dowd
JAMES BALDWIN	Alexander Clark
MISS BRAND	Lesley Woods
PAUL CLEARY	Sidney Blackmer
BOYD BENDIX	Larry Gates
JUDGE	Wynn Wright
CLEARY'S ASSISTANT	Tom Hammond
COURT CLERK	Douglas McLean
COURT STENOGRAPHER	William Hindman
COLONEL DOUGLAS	Philip Bourneuf
FRED ALSTON	Richard McMurray
FOREMAN OF THE JURY	Keith Parnell

Directed by SAM WANAMAKER

Settings and Lighting by DONALD OENSLAGER

Costumes by ANN ROTH

SYNOPSIS OF SCENES

Act One

Scene 1: The private office of Robert Sloane.
Scene 2: Some months later.
Scene 3: Some months later.

Act Two

Scene 1: A courtroom of the New York State Supreme Court.
Scene 2: Several days later.
Scene 3: One week later.
Scene 4: Robert Sloane's office. That night.

Act Three

Scene 1: The courtroom. The next morning.
Scene 2: Several days later.
Scene 3: Twelve hours later.

Act One

Late afternoon of a spring day in the private office of ROBERT SLOANE, *senior partner and trial counsel of a large law firm in New York City.*

The room is furnished in good taste, with an eye to comfort, not ostentation. There is a large walnut desk, a desk chair, a phone cabinet with several phones, book shelves, a sofa, several leather side chairs, and a large leather wing chair. A single door leads to the rest of the large suite.

CLAIRE MARSHALL, SLOANE'S *secretary, crosses to put on the desk two green passports, an envelope with airline tickets, some papers with information and data. The telephone is ringing insistently.*

CLAIRE (*Picking up the phone*) Mr. Sloane's office. No, he's not back from court yet. I'll tell him. (*Pasting stickers and attaching labels on briefcase; to* ABNER COLES, *as he enters*) You heard about the verdict . . .

COLES (*Enters, carrying some briefs*) Big. Too big. I've told him a thousand times, "Bob, for once, please, win a nice modest verdict." (*His attention is caught by the items on the desk*) Passports . . . tickets . . . itinerary . . . he's all set. Did you alert *Mrs.* Sloane?

CLAIRE Mrs. Sloane, the limousine, the luggage, all alerted and ready.

COLES Good. Now if we can sneak him past the other partners, he can be off. He needs a rest. Badly. (*She*

glances questioningly at the briefs, and he notices) This?
Just the briefs on the Walberg appeal . . . *(Feeling im-
pelled to explain)* I figured, every vacation has a few
rainy days. He might *welcome* the chance to look it over.
*(He puts them down on the desk but at the same time
notices a pile of briefs)* The Donner matter?

CLAIRE   Mr. Parker said he might "welcome the chance"
to look it over.

COLES   And the Sun-Ray Chemicals matter . . .

CLAIRE   Mr. Solomon said he might "welcome the chance"
to look it over.
    *(DAVID STRONG, SLOANE'S young assistant, enters,
    loaded down with two heavy leather cases full of
    books and exhibits)*

COLES   Where's Mr. Sloane?

DAVID   *(As he digs some papers out of the cases and puts
them on the desk)*   He just stopped to pick up something for his wife. *(He interrupts himself when he spies
something on the desk, is impressed)* Calls from the *New
York Times*, Associated Press, News International . . .
(CLAIRE turns over the message list) Too late. You know,
I can read better upside down than *other* people can
right side up.

COLES   Is that how you studied at Harvard, hanging from
a trapeze?

DAVID   If they all called this afternoon, it can be for only
one reason.

4

COLES   It happens every time he wins a big one. But news syndicates don't appoint judges.

DAVID   He should be on the bench!

COLES   Look, John Harvard, if they ever trap him in a black robe, they might as well make it a shroud.
   (ROBERT SLOANE *enters. If he is tired, he has lost neither vigor nor humor. He heard* COLES)

SLOANE   Ab . . . I may not get to be a judge. But don't bury me, either.

COLES   Congratulations . . . some verdict!
   (*The phone rings,* CLAIRE *answers. During this*)

SLOANE   Thanks. But I can tell you now, if that case'd gone one more day I don't know if I could have finished it.

CLAIRE   (*Hands over the phone*)   News International . . . they are the *most* persistent . . . third time they've called.

SLOANE   Claire, please, I'm too tired. You take it. Out there. Say that I have not been approached on any judgeship and if I were . . . well, use Mr. Coles' line about the shroud.
   (*As* CLAIRE *crosses to the door*)

COLES   Only a figure of speech. Some men can't be neutral. They have to fight or die.

SLOANE   Well, this is one day I'm fed up with fighting.

DAVID   No wonder. I counted it up only this morning . . . in the year since I've been here . . . you've been in court

5

one hundred and ninety-seven days. And when you include the nights of preparation . . .

(SLOANE *hadn't ever figured that out, so he turns, amused and surprised, to look at* DAVID)

COLES He also reads upside down and nominates judges for the Supreme Court. He is man's answer to IBM.

SLOANE Then be nice to him, Ab. One day *we'll* be appearing before *him*. (*To* DAVID) But till then, start working up a memorandum of law on excessive damages, so we'll be ready for the appeal on today's verdict.

DAVID Yes, sir!

(*As he exits,* SLOANE *goes to the desk to take vacation inventory*)

SLOANE Tickets . . . passports . . . letter of credit . . .

(*But he is interrupted by* CLAIRE, *who enters puzzled and upset*)

CLAIRE Mr. Sloane, did you make an appointment with Dennis Corcoran?

SLOANE Dennis Corcoran? I didn't even *talk* to him. I told you to tell him this morning I couldn't see him.

CLAIRE And I did. But he's out there. He and *Mrs.* Corcoran. Insisting on seeing you.

SLOANE Oh? Well, this is one day nobody makes demands on me! I'm exhausted! My vacation started ten minutes ago. Ab, you know what this is about.

COLES (*Nods, picks up an unread newspaper on desk*) If anybody called me an "immoral, yellow-bellied degenerate" who masquerades as a big brave war correspondent, I'd be looking for a good lawyer myself, today.

CLAIRE (*Starts out*) I'll get rid of them.

SLOANE No—wait—I suppose I'll have to be polite. He's at least entitled to courtesy. (COLES *nods understandingly*) Send them in. (*As* CLAIRE *goes, he calls to her*) And interrupt me in about five minutes, "remind" me I have to pick up Mrs. Sloane on the way to the airport. (COLES *starts out*) Ab, wait. I'll start with him, then you take over and explain why we can't consider taking on a case like this.

COLES Okay. (SLOANE *puts the tickets and passports into his pocket, starts to put some papers into his briefcase when* COLES *places the newspaper on his desk, folded open to a particular place.* SLOANE *picks it up, looks to* COLES, *who shrugs*) Sometimes when you're on trial you don't get to read the newspaper. That's the latest article.

SLOANE I've read it.
(*They are interrupted by* CLAIRE's *knock and the entrance of* DENNIS *and* ANITA CORCORAN)

CLAIRE Mr. Sloane . . . Mr. and Mrs. Corcoran . . .

SLOANE Of course! We've met. Several years ago. Remember? (*He holds out his hand to shake with* DENNIS) My partner . . . Mr. Coles.

DENNIS I want to apologize. You're busy, I know, and you're going away; your secretary made all that quite clear. Believe me, if I had any choice I wouldn't be here.

SLOANE   I read them all. We know exactly how you feel.

DENNIS (*Sharply*)   I don't think so! (SLOANE *is stopped by this*) Till Bendix started writing these articles about me, I used to think I knew "exactly how it felt."
   (*Digging into his pocket, he pulls out a handful of clippings and spills them onto the desk*)

ANITA   I've been begging him for weeks now to see you, Mr. Sloane. If you just lift your phone, call Boyd Bendix, or his editor at News International . . . I think your reputation alone would make them stop!

SLOANE   That's very nice to hear. But not exactly true. Besides, we'd have to know a great deal more than I could learn in a brief interview before we could even consider taking on a case like this . . .

DENNIS   Anything you have to know, just ask!

SLOANE   If you'll go along to Mr. Cole's office—

ANITA   *You're* the one who can help Dennis—please, Mr. Sloane—just a few minutes. Please?

SLOANE (*A look to AB, this won't be as easy to untangle from as he hoped, but he has no choice till that phone rings*)   Well, frankly, I've been a little puzzled from the beginning. I thought Boyd Bendix was a friend of yours.

ANITA   He was!

SLOANE   Then what do you think accounts for all this? Attacks like these, unprovoked, just don't happen.

8

ANITA (*To* DENNIS) That's what *I* said. I said, it must have been that book review!

DENNIS A brief book review that appeared in one magazine wouldn't justify all *this*!

SLOANE What book review?

DENNIS *Hangman on Horseback.* I reviewed it for *Monitor.* (SLOANE *looks puzzled*) A biography of Bendix.

SLOANE Which said?

DENNIS That Bendix might consider himself the man on horseback to solve the problems of our time . . . that he's eccentric, difficult . . . and brave only when there is no danger.

SLOANE And your review?

DENNIS I agreed with the book.

SLOANE Then these weren't exactly "unprovoked," were they? Look, Dennis, let me give you the law on libel and slander in a nutshell. You have to prove that you've been lied about, preferably unprovoked, and that you sustained damage. Can you prove all that? Especially the part about damage? A man in your position, with your income? Can you? (*The phone rings*) Yes? . . . Thank you, Claire. (*Hangs up*) I'm afraid I really must—

ANITA (*Interrupting. To* DENNIS) Tell him why you finally agreed to come here today.

DENNIS Nita, please!

ANITA Tell him! Because if you don't, I will!

DENNIS   This is an article of mine. (*He hands* SLOANE *the folded rumpled script envelope.* SLOANE *takes it, opens it, looks at the title*) I sent it in on Tuesday. Yesterday I got a call from Fred Alston . . .

SLOANE   Alston?

DENNIS   My editor at *Monitor*. Said for me to meet him at the restaurant, *not* at the office, which was strange, but I did. When I got there, I could see that Fred had had a few. He drinks a little. But today he was smashed. I couldn't understand why, till he reached under his chair, fumbled for something, and held it out to me.

SLOANE   (*Indicating the article*)   Your story?

DENNIS   Then he just got up and started out. I went after him, but he kept trying to turn away, till I grabbed him, and I said, "Fred, what the hell are you trying to tell me?" For a minute I thought he was going to cry. Finally he mumbled something about "questions from advertisers, letters from readers about why we keep publishing you." "They're scared," he said, "—the top brass is scared —you've been 'Bendixed' and they don't want trouble." I said, "Fred, you don't believe that garbage, do you?" And he said—

SLOANE   (*Anticipating him*)   "They wouldn't print it, if there wasn't some truth in it."

DENNIS (*Taken aback, he nods*)   That's right.

SLOANE   "But don't worry, Denny, it'll all blow over." That too?

DENNIS Yes. How did you . . .

SLOANE It always "blows over." At least that's what they say.

ANITA Somebody's got to stop this man!

SLOANE Who? You? Alone? You're hot. You're in trouble. And because you are, everybody who knows you wants to be dissociated from you, be safe, clean, antiseptic.

DENNIS Not my friends!

SLOANE Like Fred Alston . . .

ANITA He said he'd do anything he could!

SLOANE Don't bet on it.

DENNIS (*Pointing to the news clips*) I only know one thing! They can't tell lies like this about a man and get away with it!
  (*Again, the phone rings,* SLOANE *turns to answer it, unable, however, to escape looking at* COLES)

SLOANE Yes, Claire? Oh, yes, yes . . . well . . . well, would you call Mrs. Sloane and ask her to pick me up here instead. That'll give us another fifteen minutes . . . just do as I said! Yes! And send David Strong in here, please. (*He hangs up, more annoyed with himself than anyone else, because he's become enmeshed*) Now you're going to see a nice, bright young man come through that door. He's going to help me prove something, something I think you ought to learn, now. (DAVID *enters.* SLOANE

deliberately does not introduce DAVID *and the* CORCORANS)
David, ever see any of these?
(*He hands* DAVID *the clippings*)

DAVID (*Primly dogmatic, he puts down the clippings*) I
don't read Bendix.

SLOANE Well, read him now. Out loud.

DAVID (*Puzzled, but obeying orders*) Yes, sir. "In recent
days I have been accosted in public places by friends of
that hulky, bulky chunk of Irish blubber, one Dennis
Corcoran. Their plaints are of one long alcoholic note,
'What am I trying to do to this big brave drinking buddy
of theirs?' As a diligent working reporter I felt it my duty
to probe deeper into the mud of Corcoran's past life."
(DAVID *looks up*)

SLOANE Go on!

DAVID "I accuse Dennis Corcoran of having nothing but
gas where a man should have guts. Of letting high-school
kids die to win a war out of which Corcoran earned more
than a million dollars. Of selling his country and its freedom down the river by picking up the Commie chant,
the Moscow-manufactured demand for a second front..."

DENNIS (*Interrupting*) Mr. Sloane, what's the purpose of
this?

SLOANE (*To* DAVID) Go on!

DAVID (*More tentative now than before*) "... Any publication should consider carefully the effect on its cus-
tomers, who might not subscribe to the words of this

drunken, immoral, yellow-bellied degenerate who tried to give us the impression that he was a fearless war correspondent."

SLOANE What do you think?

DAVID Legally, sir? It's libelous, of course.

SLOANE For the moment, never mind the law! What do *you* think?

DAVID Well, that part about not wanting the war to be over . . . that's certainly not true!

SLOANE And the part about the second front?

DAVID Everyone knows Mr. Corcoran's record as a war correspondent . . . he *was* for a second front.

SLOANE So what Bendix says is true.

DAVID Not exactly.

SLOANE Is it false?

DAVID I couldn't exactly say that.

SLOANE Which is precisely the same as saying "Maybe it's true." If it's not, deny it! Call it a lie!

DAVID Well, I . . .
     (*He is unable to reply*)

SLOANE Thanks, David. (DAVID *exits*) There's part of your answer. Sure. There's a law that says they can't *do* this to a man . . . but the process by which that law is en-

13

forced is difficult, very technical, highly uncertain, and extremely costly. Why, from the first day of preparation through the motions, appeals, the trial and the appeals from the trial, it can take five years, maybe even longer! And cost thousands of dollars!

ANITA We don't care what it costs!

SLOANE Even if it destroys him forever? (*This hadn't occurred to her before.* SLOANE *lets it sink in, then*) Libel is one lawsuit in which the plaintiff is on the defensive all the time.

DENNIS I'm willing to *be* on the defensive! I've got nothing to hide!

> (SLOANE *picks up the crumpled newspaper clip and straightens it out*)

SLOANE "Their plaints are of one long *alcoholic* note . . . this big brave *drinking* buddy of theirs . . ." What do you say to that, Dennis?

DENNIS Sure, I drink, so what! But I'm not a drunkard! (*Ripping the clipping out of* SLOANE's *hand*) I'm not a "drunken, immoral, yellow-bellied degenerate who tried to give us the impression that he was a fearless war correspondent."

SLOANE Ever been afraid, Dennis?

DENNIS Of *course* I've been afraid!

SLOANE Then you're not fearless, are you?

DENNIS I never said I was! *He* said I tried to give that impression.

SLOANE   That's the point! He tells a lie about you and *your* reputation is in question. Not *his!* Do you know what it means to have your reputation in question in a lawsuit?

DENNIS   He lied about me and I can prove it!

SLOANE   Prove that you're not immoral? Drunken? Cowardly? How, Dennis? Imagine you were Christ Himself on the witness stand being cross-examined. (*He turns to an empty chair to use as a witness*) "Now, sir, you say you are a carpenter? Yet isn't it a fact that from the ages of thirty to thirty-three, three whole years, you didn't work at *anything,* just wandered the countryside as a vagrant? And during that time, did you drink? Only wine. Uh huh. And did you ever commit assault against a group of moneychangers? And did you have frequent contact with a known prostitute? I didn't ask you why! Just answer the question! You *did!* Thank you." (*Then turning to* DENNIS) How do you think *you'd* make out? What are *you* going to say when Bendix's lawyer asks *you* about that woman?
(DENNIS *is surprised that* SLOANE *knows anything about her*)

DENNIS (*Guiltily exchanging a look with* ANITA)   How did you . . . That was all over before I married Nita! Look— *she's* married, too—and doesn't even *live* in this country.

SLOANE   They might bring it up. And all they'd have to discover is that you're sensitive about it. (*Taking account of* DENNIS' *puzzlement*) No, I didn't know. But every normal man has had at least one serious relationship like that. Now, imagine what an outfit like News International could do to you, with investigators, private detectives . . .

ANITA (*Asking more than knowing*)   Dennis has nothing to hide!

DENNIS   I'm not a saint. Never said I was. But damn it . . . I'm not going to keep quiet in the face of this! I can *prove* he's a liar!

SLOANE   Dennis, I advise you not to start jousting with the most powerful news syndicate in the world. When they fight you, they're fighting *everyone* who's ever going to contemplate suing them for libel. They've got millions to spend, batteries of the best lawyers, on retainer. Have you? No. In fact, no successful lawyer is going to take a case like yours on a contingent fee. Because even if you win, you might well win nothing.

DENNIS (*A pause. To* SLOANE)   Are you saying don't take the risk, don't go ahead with this case?

SLOANE   It won't be just a case! It'll be a way of life. It'll live with you, twenty-four hours a day. You'll wake up in the middle of the night asking yourself imaginary questions, giving answers more brilliant than any you'll ever give in a courtroom. I know. I ask my best questions between three and four in the morning. You don't want to live like that. Believe me.
    (*He turns back to his desk*)

DENNIS (*Resentfully*)   Come on, darling. Well, I'm sorry I troubled you . . .

SLOANE I told you the truth. (*Turning back*) Did you expect more than that?

DENNIS Frankly, yes! But never mind—I'm sorry I "delayed" your vacation.
(*He turns away, starts for the door*)

COLES Now, just a minute!

DENNIS Sorry, my mistake. I guess I came to the wrong man.

COLES Unless you've been through a fight like this, don't judge!

SLOANE Ab!

COLES He asked for it! You know you're not the first man was libeled and wanted to sue. We knew a young lawyer once who wanted to fight for justice, like you. In fact that's how he got into trouble. Back in the Thirties he'd "joined," marched, picketed, spoke, ran mimeographs. Till the New Deal. And a job in one of the new government agencies. Soon he was looking at the world as a place to live—not picket—to meet a girl, settle down, have kids—*until* one of those investigations came along. Called, he appeared. Asked, he answered. Till it became clear they didn't want answers, only self-condemnation. So his resignation was requested. And given. Then a newspaper printed his name as one of a group of "subversives" who'd been rooted out of the government. Now —at last—a chance to go into court—to fight back—like you. So he came to Bob. And because they'd been friends, Bob took it on. And presented a damned good case. Till the defense took over on cross-examination. They asked his client, "Have you ever been friendly with the head of the government department you worked in?" "Yes." "Is he the same man who was later arrested and pleaded guilty to accosting another man in the Union Station in Washington?" It was a mistake for the judge even to admit the question. But suddenly, from that moment on, it was no longer a case about the right to be immune from libel, but a desperate battle to prove his client wasn't a homosexual. An issue that had nothing to do with the case. A charge that had nothing to do with his client. Bob finally won his vindication. But in the process, the man lost his wife and family, had a breakdown, spent four years in a sanitarium. He had *fought,* and won. Losing is even worse.

SLOANE They'll smear you in their papers, drag you through the courts for years, till you wish to God you never started this.

DENNIS Mr. Sloane, are you trying to tell me that our kind of justice depends on size or number of dollars? Because if it doesn't, why is Robert Sloane telling me to run hide?

SLOANE Dennis, listen to me . . .

DENNIS As far as I'm concerned, running and hiding are not dignified occupations for any human being!

SLOANE Now, *listen* to me!

DENNIS The fight Mr. Coles was talking about was twenty years ago. You aren't the same man! Why?

18

SLOANE (*Just about in control of himself*) It's just as necessary to warn a client about the practical realities of his case as about the law.

DENNIS Or would you rather represent News International than me? Is that it? Because they pay better? And then you can have your principles and eat 'em too. And should your conscience get a little restive you can make a speech or write a check for a donation and all's well again. But all the time you know . . . deep down inside, you know that what this represents (*Brandishes the clippings*) is more important than any fee there is! Or any speech or any donation. (*He turns and goes to the door, stops, turns back*) Forgive me, if I spoke too loud, or too frankly. I regret one thing . . . that the Robert Sloane of twenty years ago, the one who didn't know so damn much about "practical realities," isn't around any more. He's the lawyer I need!

　　(DENNIS *slams out.* SLOANE *recovers, dares to reach for the crumpled clippings, fingers them but has not the heart to read them again*)

COLES A man who's hurt, frightened, says things he doesn't mean . . .

SLOANE (*Suddenly*) "Some men have to fight or die." What did you mean by that?

　　(COLES, *not used to such an attack, looks at* SLOANE, *puzzled*)

COLES It was only a chance remark. It didn't mean anything. (SLOANE *can't help staring at the door through which* DENNIS *and* ANITA *exited. To divert his attention*

COLES *starts again*) Now, Bob, you don't have much time and we have a few things to go over . . . (*Hefting the briefs as he talks*) In order of importance . . . the Walberg matter . . . the Donner matter . . . Sun-Ray Chemicals . . .

SLOANE What about the Sloane matter? (*Taken unaware, COLES is momentarily puzzled*) What about the matter of Robert Sloane?

COLES (*Evading*) Bob, you're only one man. You can't take every case.

SLOANE He wasn't asking me to take every case! Only one case. His. And I turned him down. Why?

COLES Now, Bob . . .

SLOANE Ab, level with me! Was he telling me the truth? Am I buying myself off with fat contributions, speeches, "nice causes"? Have I caught the bug? Am I dying of success? (COLES *does not answer. They stare at each other a long moment*) Thanks, Ab. For not lying to me. How long have you noticed it?
(*Before* COLES *can answer*, CLAIRE *enters suddenly*)

CLAIRE I'm sorry, Mr. Sloane, but they're *both* on the phone now . . . the *New York Times* and News International . . . and they're very insistent. They want to talk to you directly.

SLOANE News International? . . . What line are they on?

CLAIRE Four.
(SLOANE *lifts the phone*)

SLOANE   This is Sloane. Oh? Well, thank you. Your sug-
gestion is very flattering. But I'm afraid I won't have
time to serve on the bench right now.
(He is interrupted by DAVID *entering to get the
briefcases and briefs and explain hastily)*

DAVID   Sorry, but Mrs. Sloane and the car are downstairs!

SLOANE *(Hand over the mouthpiece)*   See if you can stop
Corcoran at the elevator. Chase him down the block if
you have to. But bring him back here! *(As* DAVID *hesitates,* COLES *turns him about and shoves him out, and*
SLOANE *returns to speaking into the phone)* Yes, yes,
it's a new case. The client? Well, I can't reveal that at
the moment . . . But believe me, you'll be the first to
know!

            Blackout

Scene 2

Months later, the afternoon of a winter day. SLOANE'S
*office is strewn with books, files, memos—indicating much
preparation and research has been going on.* ABNER COLES
*enters, jacket off, glasses up on his forehead, and puts down
some papers on one of the many stacks on the table. He is
followed by* BALDWIN, *a graying, dignified member of the
firm, who is finishing what has been a not particularly
happy argument with* COLES.

BALDWIN   Don't misunderstand me, Ab.

COLES (*Slightly sarcastic*)   Of course not, Jim . . .

BALDWIN   We're running a law office, not a Legal Aid
Society! Oh, it's not the money. I'm as quick to recognize
a public responsibility as the next man.

COLES   For once, I'd like to see that "next man" everybody
keeps comparing himself to.

BALDWIN (*Sharply*)   If it wasn't for this antitrust matter
we never would have got Standard's business in the first
place!

COLES   You mean if it wasn't for Bob.

BALDWIN   We share his glory. And we're willing to share
his risks. Even on cases that cost us a lot of money. But
Standard has a right to ask why he isn't out in Chicago
arguing this appeal for them.

COLES   Because he's been in London on business.

BALDWIN (*Indicating the littered desk*) "Corcoran business." That's precisely the point. If he'd treat that Corcoran case like any other, I wouldn't mind. But, as it is, we'd be a lot better off without it! For six months we have had half the staff tied up with it. Parker complained to me only yesterday . . .

COLES (*Interrupting*)   Jim, if Standard wants Bob to argue their appeal, they'll have to wait!

BALDWIN   It seems they don't have to. (*Indicating a paper he holds*) Their last letter mentions a possible substitution of attorneys.
(*Shocked,* COLES *takes the letter as the door opens and* CLAIRE *escorts* DENNIS *and* ANITA *into the room*)

CLAIRE   Excuse me—

DENNIS (*Casual greeting*)   Mr. Baldwin . . .

BALDWIN   Good afternoon . . . Claire, I'd like to have a minute with Mr. Sloane when he comes in.
(*He exits*)

ANITA   Has something gone wrong?

COLES   Nothing's gone wrong. Bob only called from the airport and asked that we have you and Dennis here when he arrived.

DENNIS   How did he make out?

COLES   He didn't say. Now just relax, he'll be here any moment.

23

(COLES *exits to catch* BALDWIN. ANITA *and* DENNIS
*are left alone. Their uneasiness becomes manifest
when* DENNIS *lights a cigarette, takes a deep puff
and only then realizes he didn't offer her one. He
holds out his to her*)

DENNIS Sorry, darling . . .

ANITA (*She doesn't take it, instead asks thoughtfully*)
Why would he rush here right from the airport? What's
so urgent?

DENNIS It wasn't because of anything he discovered in
England about me.

ANITA Darling, I didn't say . . .

DENNIS No, but you're thinking it. "She" lives in London.

ANITA I wasn't thinking anything of the sort! And I'm
not accusing you of anything. In fact . . . (*Realizing how
tense she's suddenly become, she tries now to make light
of it, smiles*) Good God, are we having an argument
about this . . . after what we said . . .
(*He goes to her, takes her gently in his arms*)

DENNIS What happened to Bob's friend is *not* going to
happen to us. Remember what we agreed . . .

ANITA No secrets . . .

DENNIS *And* no arguments.

ANITA No arguments.
(*He kisses her gently. They are interrupted by*
SLOANE *entering.* DAVID *follows carrying* SLOANE'S

24

briefcase and attaché case both ticketed with airline tags. COLES *follows carrying some blue-backed legal documents and* BALDWIN's *letter on top*)

ANITA Bob, what happened? How did it go?

SLOANE Fine. Just fine! (*Referring to their kiss*) And it looks like everything's going just fine here, too.

DENNIS Did you see Montgomery . . . Mountbatten . . . ?

SLOANE Saw them both. Even Sir Winston himself.

ANITA What are they going to do to *help?*

SLOANE None of the three can come over and testify . . . protocol. So we'll get their depositions. But we *will* have one witness. Colonel Douglas.

DENNIS That Scotch son-of-a-bitch, you could always depend on him! Oh, sorry, that *Scots* son-of-a-bitch. He's very finicky about that.

SLOANE (*Turning more serious now*) Ab . . . the copies? (*As* COLES *hands them to him*) Bendix's legal answer to our complaint. Served on us yesterday. Ab called me in London, read it to me.

ANITA That why you came back so suddenly?

SLOANE (*Suddenly*) Dennis, does Bendix *know* something about you, about your *past,* that I don't?

DENNIS (*Taken aback*) No! Certainly not!

SLOANE Because if there *is* anything like that and I *know* about it *now,* I can fight it. But if I'm taken by surprise, we don't have a chance!

25

ANITA   Do you think Dennis lied to you?

SLOANE   After *this*, I have a right to question everything!

DENNIS   What do you mean?

SLOANE   Looks like a legal answer . . . reads like a legal answer . . . but then suddenly it isn't an answer at all. It's an attack! A new attack with new charges! (*Reading from the papers*) "Defendant further alleges that plaintiff has, on a number of occasions, wenched about in public with a certain unidentified woman, without regard for public morals or the immediate presence of other persons, including minors . . ."

DENNIS   You don't believe that! (*To* ANITA) He must be out of his mind!

SLOANE   ". . . from the safety of a highly protected place, plaintiff watched as wave after wave of young Allied soldiers went to their bloody death . . ." (*Finding another*) ". . . plaintiff used his position as a journalist of great prominence to influence American public opinion in favor of Communist Russia."

DENNIS   Hell, he's not going back to that old malarkey, is he?

SLOANE   If what you say is true, this is a document *full* of lies! All right, *why*?

DENNIS   I don't *know* why!

ANITA (*Indignantly*)   How can the law let a man tell such lies about another man and call it a legal document? How?

26

COLES (*Handing* SLOANE *a sheaf of papers*) Wait till you're confronted with Section Three Thirty-eight, if you want to know how a man can lie about another man legally.

ANITA Three Thirty-eight?
(*A door knock interrupts. The door opens.* BALDWIN *enters, carrying a newspaper folded open to a particular column*)

BALDWIN Sorry, Bob, but my secretary just got back from lunch and showed me this . . . I thought you ought to see it at once.

SLOANE What is it?

BALDWIN Boyd Bendix's column today. "This same Corcoran went to Moscow and used his position as a journalist of great prominence to influence public opinion in favor of Communist—"
(SLOANE *interrupts by taking the paper from his hands and placing it alongside the legal answer on the desk*)

SLOANE I've practiced law a long time but this is the dirtiest . . . let me show you what they've done . . . they're real cute. They set this forth in their answer first, to get legal privilege. (*Showing the legal document*) And then Bendix reprints it in here, in his column.

COLES (*To* DENNIS *and* ANITA) A newspaper can reprint any legal document with complete immunity.

SLOANE (*Lifting the phone*) Get me Paul Cleary! (*He begins to hang up, then hesitates and stops*) No, never

mind. (*Hangs up, saying to* COLES *and* BALDWIN) We've
done business with Paul Cleary before. Does *this* strike
you as Cleary? (*Indicating the answer*) Or *any* sound,
ethical lawyer?

BALDWIN (*To* DENNIS *and* ANITA)   An attorney defending
a suit like this should apologize, offer to retract, if only
to emerge from it with the least possible risk.

SLOANE   Who knows that better than Cleary? Yet here he
is attacking. Maliciously! Conclusion? Maybe this isn't
Cleary.

COLES   Bendix?

SLOANE   *He's* running this defense! And because he's their
prize columnist, News International is *letting* him run it.
(*Thinking*) So Bendix wants to play lawyer, does he?
(*Suddenly to* DENNIS) Dennis, when you leave here,
take a copy of this answer. Study it! Learn it by heart if
you have to. But nail down every lie in here with facts,
dates, witnesses, provable truth. Now, two things . . .
first, your friend . . . (*Groping for identification*) your
editor . . .

DENNIS   Fred—Fred Alston . . .

SLOANE   Did you get the statement?

DENNIS   Not yet.

SLOANE   Well, keep after him! Get it! Remember what I
told you . . . if we prove the whole case and can't prove
damages we can wind up with only six cents. So get
Alston's statement! Now, *second* . . . think of something

John Randolph, M'el Dowd, Alexander Clark, Van Heflin, and Joseph Julian, as DENNIS CORCORAN, ANITA CORCORAN, JAMES BALDWIN, ROBERT SLOANE, and ABNER COLES

particularly insulting, *and* truthful, to say in public or in print about Boyd Bendix.

(*Even* COLES *and* BALDWIN *are startled at this*)

DENNIS   That's not difficult.

SLOANE   Something strong enough to provoke him into *counter*claiming, into suing *you*? (DENNIS' *surprise makes him add thoughtfully*) A little insurance . . . just in case . . .

DENNIS   In case what?

(SLOANE *waves off his question*)

SLOANE   Now, if the rest of you don't mind, I'd like some time alone with Dennis . . .

(COLES *and* ANITA *start out*)

ANITA   I'll wait for you at home, darling . . .

BALDWIN   (*He does not move.* SLOANE, *then* DENNIS, *become uncomfortably aware of that*)   I'd like a minute, Bob. Surely, you can spare it.

SLOANE   Of course, Jim. Denny . . .

(COLES *holds the door for* DENNIS, *exits last looking at* BALDWIN, *concerned about what he might say*)

SLOANE   Okay, Jim . . . shoot!

BALDWIN   I didn't want them (*Indicating the* CORCORANS) to know . . . that's why I said my *secretary* brought this in. (SLOANE *picks up the newspaper*) Went down and got it myself. *After* Farrell called to tell me about it.

SLOANE   *Pete* Farrell—Metropolitan Construction—why would he call about . . .

BALDWIN (*Taking the newspaper*)   Bendix writes like an insurance-company contract. You have to read him *all the way through*. Listen to his last line. "However I feel about Dennis Corcoran, I say, 'Thank God for the American system of justice that allows him to be represented by the *same firm of lawyers* that represents some of the largest corporations in our country.' " Subtle. But very, very clear.

(*The threat makes* SLOANE *take back the paper to see it for himself*)

SLOANE   "Hooray for the American system." As long as we don't try to make it work, hmm?

BALDWIN   That's not what *Pete* called to say. (SLOANE *looks at* BALDWIN *sharply*) Bob, this article will appear today in Washington, Chicago, Boston, Detroit . . .

SLOANE   And every *other* city where we have important clients . . .

BALDWIN   I'm not asking you to think about the firm or your partners . . .

SLOANE (*Interrupting*)   This was the first time I ever took on a case without consulting all of you, wasn't it?

BALDWIN   All we stand to lose is money. But News International can be pretty vindictive. So any hopes or ambitions you ever had about being on the bench . . .

SLOANE   Right now I have only one ambition. To win this case!

BALDWIN   One thing sure. This means that News International, Cleary, they're not scared. Else they wouldn't be giving Bendix his head. Why, to them this isn't a lawsuit. It's a game. A joke! You might think about that, too, if winning is what's on your mind.

(BALDWIN *exits,* SLOANE *picks up the paper, thoughtfully.* DENNIS *enters*)

DENNIS   Mr. Baldwin gave you some bad news, didn't he?

SLOANE   No. Now, sit down, Dennis . . . for the next few hours I want to learn everything you know about Boyd Bendix. Because if he *is* going to run this case, I want to know him inside and out, what he likes, hates, fears and loves. Everything! Now, start! Fill me in!

DENNIS   Well, the strange thing is, he was actually a good Joe . . . I mean, before he got to be a celebrity he was one of the boys, *and* one of the best damn newspapermen around. And still is! On opposite sides of the political fence from most of us, but it didn't interfere. He'd hang around with us, do his share of drinking . . .

SLOANE   And wenching around? (DENNIS *reacts*) The word he used in there about you.

DENNIS   You'd be wasting your time looking for anything like that with him.

SLOANE   Why?

DENNIS   One thing about Ben, once he got married . . . at least, once Emily had that . . . we never did know if it was a miscarriage or a premature birth . . .

SLOANE   I see.

31

DENNIS   And when Emily wasn't able to have any children . . . it brought them closer together, somehow. So
if Ben's anything, he's moral.

SLOANE   *Too* moral, maybe? (DENNIS *looks puzzled*)
Afraid, possibly, to give any other impression?

DENNIS   Even after Emily was invalided, he never played
around.

SLOANE   Invalid? Since when? I'd never heard.

DENNIS   Ben keeps his own life pretty private.

SLOANE   (*Thinking*)   An invalid. And he never played
around . . . *that's* unusual, isn't it?

DENNIS   Not for a man like Ben.

SLOANE   Why?

DENNIS   He's . . . he's just that kind of man.

SLOANE   *What* kind?

DENNIS   Rigid, firm, puritanical. Above suspicion or criticism.

SLOANE   My father used to say, "Jews are perverse people.
We go to synagogue on Yom Kippur to square our accounts with God. But do we recite our virtues? No. Only
our faults. Why? Because a man's testimony about his
own virtues is always suspect. But more important, because it is indecent for a man not to have some faults.
Else he would be competing with God." So, your friend
Bendix competes with God, does he?

DENNIS   I'll say this for him. He's sincere. Whatever makes his wheels spin the way they do sometimes, Ben really believes in what he does.

SLOANE   By the way, you'd better start cultivating a new habit from now on. (DENNIS *reacts, puzzled*) The habit of *not* calling him Ben . . .

DENNIS   But I've always . . .

SLOANE   (*Interrupting*)   From now on, he's the most dangerous enemy you have. Never forget it! So no more "Ben"!

DENNIS   Okay.

SLOANE   Now, start from the beginning and tell me everything you know about Boyd Bendix! . . . Puritan!

Blackout

SCENE 3

The office, some months later. As the lights come up
COLES *is preparing for the examination by moving chairs to*
face the desk. CLAIRE *assists with the ash trays. A young*
woman, the stenotypist, in street clothes, with a hat, enters
carrying her stenotype machine, which she will set up.
CLAIRE *exits.*

COLES Miss Brand. (*He indicates where she will sit*)
You'll be sitting there.

MISS BRAND Yes, sir.
(*She goes to her place, starts to open and use the*
machine to warm up. As she does, SLOANE *enters*
from another office)

COLES (*Introducing*) Miss Brand . . .

SLOANE Good morning, Miss Brand.

COLES (*Handing* SLOANE *a sheaf of papers*) Your notes.
Your list of questions for the examination.

SLOANE Any word from Cleary about Bendix?

COLES Not yet.

SLOANE This time he'd better be here!
(*The phone rings.* COLES *answers*)

COLES Yes? Oh? Send them in! (*Hangs up*) Well, they're
here. But it took a court order to get him here.

34

(*The door opens and* CLAIRE *shows* PAUL CLEARY *in*)

CLAIRE Mr. Cleary.
(*She exits.* CLEARY, *a dapper, dignified man in his fifties, enters*)

CLEARY Bob . . .

SLOANE Paul . . . (*They start to shake hands till* SLOANE *realizes*) Paul, where is he? I warned you that this time . . .

CLEARY Bob, please. No need to be upset. We're friends. I wouldn't pull anything on you.

SLOANE Let's get one thing straight, Paul. We can be friends. That's fine . . . on other days . . . in *other* cases.

CLEARY I'm a lawyer, Bob. Like you.

SLOANE Are you going to justify what your client did about getting Corcoran's speaking engagement canceled at the veterans' convention? That cost Corcoran a twenty-five-hundred-dollar fee!

CLEARY Sorry, Bob, I'll caution him again.

SLOANE If your client isn't here in five minutes, I'll move to declare him in default!

CLEARY He called and said he might be a few minutes late, on a matter having to do with this case. (SLOANE *reacts with open skepticism*) Bob, we've known each other too many years . . .

SLOANE Not under circumstances like these!

(The door opens and BOYD BENDIX *enters, smiling, tall, once blond, his hair is now sandy-gray. He is lean, in excellent physical shape)*

BENDIX   I beg your pardon, but I was told to go right in. Paul . . .

CLEARY   Ben . . . this is . . .

BENDIX   Mr. Sloane . . . recognize you from your pictures in the press.
(He approaches to shake hands)

SLOANE   Mr. Bendix . . . it's my duty to warn you, this is as much a proceeding in law as if we were in a court-room.

BENDIX *(Pleasantly)*   That's still no reason *not* to shake hands, is it?
(They shake)

SLOANE   Swear him in, Miss Brand.

BENDIX *(Charmingly putting his hand on the Bible and raising his right hand)*   Am I doing it right, Miss Brand?

MISS BRAND   Do you solemnly swear to tell the truth, the whole truth and nothing but the truth, so help you God?

BENDIX *(Joining her)*   . . . so help me God.

SLOANE   Mr. Bendix . . .
(Indicating a chair near the desk)

BENDIX   Do you mind if I stand?
(SLOANE resents it)

36

CLEARY There's really no *legal* reason why he can't, is there?

SLOANE All right, Paul. (BENDIX *acknowledges that with a polite nod and a gesture meaning, "Take over, I'm in your hands"*) Now, sir, you are Boyd Bendix, columnist for and co-defendant in this action with News International?

BENDIX The very same.

SLOANE Now, Mr. Bendix, I show you a copy of a newspaper column and ask you to identify it for us.

BENDIX (*Takes the clipping, looks at it*) Yes, this is my column of today's date.

SLOANE Did you, when you wrote this column, know that under court order you would be required to appear here today for an examination before trial?

BENDIX (*Enjoying some semantic exercise*) If you're asking me whether I wrote this in anger over being forced to attend this . . . this legal hog-sticking . . . the answer is no. *But* if you are asking me if this column was written to prove that no one . . . no lawyer, no judge, no court . . . can silence Bendix by any order or threat, why the answer is yes, I wrote *this* with this examination in mind.

CLEARY He doesn't mean to be argumentative, Bob. That's just his style . . .

BENDIX Paul, don't apologize for me.

CLEARY Ben . . .

BENDIX   We might as well have this out now! There won't be another chance.

SLOANE   Mr. Bendix, get one thing straight. You'll appear *every* time and at *every* place the court says you should, until we have the information we need.

BENDIX *(Smiling)*   I wouldn't be too sure of that.

SLOANE *(Provoked, but returning to the examination)* Now I read to you from your column of today's date . . . "this same Dennis Corcoran . . . who disported himself in the nude in the presence of others . . . performed sexual vulgarities of all sorts . . . was a spectator at debauchery in which partners of different colors engaged in drunken orgies which would make Nero a neophyte at nudity by comparison . . ." Do I read it correctly?

BENDIX   That part about Nero . . . read it again.

SLOANE   ". . . which would make Nero a neophyte at nudity . . ."

BENDIX   Oh, yes.

SLOANE   That's precisely the way I read it the *first* time.

BENDIX   I wanted to hear it again. It's such a good phrase.

SLOANE *(Irritated, but he continues)*   Where and on what specific occasions did these alleged orgies take place?

BENDIX   In the home, on the grounds and lake of the estate of one Eliot Andrews.

SLOANE   Eliot Andrews being the writer, columnist, personality . . .

BENDIX (*Taking it up before* SLOANE *can finish*) . . . radical, Communist, race-defiling, food-stuffing, whiskey-sucking slob. Yes.

SLOANE   I call your attention to the fact that you're characterizing a dead man and a one-time friend of yours.

BENDIX   You don't call it to *my* attention at all! You're saying it so that the stenographer will get it down and it will come to the attention of *others*.

SLOANE   Now, sir, you say that Eliot Andrews and his wife allowed such conduct even though they had young children of their own living in the house?

BENDIX   Andrews was one of those free-thinkers . . . If you want to teach your children about sex just let 'em watch. These days that's considered progressive. Kentucky mountaineers've been doing it for years.

CLEARY   One moment, Bob . . . off the record? (SLOANE *motions to* MISS BRAND *to stop*) I would like to talk to my client for a moment, privately.

SLOANE   All right.
(CLEARY *rises, motioning to* BENDIX, *who follows him to a corner of the room where they engage in a brief whispered conversation.* BENDIX *and* CLEARY *then return to the center of the room*)

CLEARY   Still off the record? (SLOANE *nods*) Bob, I knew there was something strange . . . the way this examination was going . . . I think you're entitled to know what it is.

BENDIX   It's a mistake, Paul!

39

CLEARY This time take my advice, Ben! (BENDIX *resigns himself, though he is actually happy to be forced into this position*) Bob . . . this case has been settled!

SLOANE What did you say?

CLEARY Settled. And on a very logical basis . . . henceforth neither plaintiff nor defendant will ever again refer to or write about one another in public. And this suit will be dropped.

SLOANE By whom?

CLEARY That's where he was . . . why he was late . . .

SLOANE You were meeting with Dennis Corcoran . . . this morning?

BENDIX This morning I received a phone call from *Mrs.* Corcoran. She asked to meet me.

SLOANE I don't believe you, Bendix.

BENDIX (*Amused*) Sloane, you think you're just about the smartest lawyer around, don't you? With your transparent strategy! "Get Bendix to sue. Get Bendix's character in issue, too." Right? Well, we saw through it! And still we counterclaimed. Why? Because Bendix has nothing to hide! (*Turning suddenly on* CLEARY) You were for backing off, rolling with the punch . . . for my sake? No! For News International! Well, a corporation may not have any pride but *I* do!

CLEARY Ben . . . please . . .

BENDIX And now we've got this damned thing settled, thanks to *me*. (*Turning to* SLOANE) You know, I'm really sorry this isn't going to trial. I was itching to get into that courtroom against you. Against Corcoran. To say, look at Bendix. Nine years older than Corcoran but tough as the day he was twenty-two. Not debauched or drunk. Not part of that soft, fashionable elite of the intellect which would undermine this country with Freud on the one hand and Marx on the other. (*As though anticipating an interruption from* SLOANE, *he holds up his hand, smiles*) Don't tell me. I know. Corcoran is no card-carrying Communist. Which is *exactly* what makes him so dangerous. Sloane, don't you see, the enemy dare not invade us from without so they try to destroy us from within. Through tools, pawns, cat's-paws like Dennis Corcoran, who do their work but don't carry their mark. The same kind of treachery we find in the Old Book. When the Patriarch Jacob . . . (*To* SLOANE) One of *your* co-religionists, I believe . . .

SLOANE   Maybe even a blood relative.

BENDIX   "The hands are the hands of Esau. But the voice is the voice of Jacob." I say, the voice is the voice of Corcoran! But the hand is the hand of Communism!
(*The outer door is suddenly flung open and* DENNIS CORCORAN *and his wife* ANITA *enter.* DENNIS *is enraged,* ANITA *tearful. For an instant* CORCORAN *and* BENDIX *face each other*)

BENDIX   Dennis! Denny . . .

DENNIS   (*Low and intense*)   Bob, get this bastard out of here!

BENDIX   *She* came to *me*, pleading to call it off.

41

DENNIS (*Moving close to* BENDIX) Bob . . . get him out!
(BALDWIN *enters to investigate the noise, stands at the door*)

SLOANE Dennis!

BENDIX I say, "Hate the sin, not the sinner." I'm glad to let you off the hook, Denny.

SLOANE Paul, get your client out of here! This examination is over.

CLEARY Come on, Ben!

BENDIX (*To* DENNIS) Your wife has more sense than you. She knows when to quit!
(CLEARY *is urging* BENDIX *out. At the same time, to* SLOANE)

CLEARY Believe me, Bob, I didn't know anything about this.

BENDIX (*Summoning* CLEARY) Paul!
(*They exit*)

SLOANE That will be all for now. Thank you, Miss Brand.
(MISS BRAND *exits*)

ANITA I'm sorry, Bob, I know I shouldn't have done it.

SLOANE Did you sign anything?

ANITA No. I didn't even say I could *agree*.

SLOANE (*To* DENNIS, *interrupting her*) Did *you* know she was going to see him?

DENNIS I had no idea.

ANITA I did it on my own. But I couldn't help it! Once I saw that letter this morning . . .

SLOANE What letter?

DENNIS Canceling my speaking engagement. Like a damn fool, I left it out . . .

ANITA Dennis was still asleep. I got up, went into the den, saw that letter and I thought, Why? Why is that man hounding him? How long will it go on? Till Dennis is completely destroyed? I said to myself, If I *face* him, make him *realize* the crime he was committing against Dennis—against us—he'll stop! After all, he's a human being. If I reasoned with him, appealed to him, pleaded . . . I didn't give a damn about my pride— (*Starting to cry*) I couldn't stand to see what was happening to Dennis . . . and to us . . .
    (*She has completely broken on the last.* DENNIS *takes her in his arms*)

DENNIS Darling . . . please . . . don't cry. Please. Nobody blames you. And he won't destroy us, I promise you that.
    (SLOANE *and* COLES *exchange looks, this is no good for the case or* DENNIS *and* ANITA)

SLOANE Dennis, you'd better take her home now. We'll talk about this later.

ANITA (*Recovering*) You can . . . talk about it now. I'm sorry . . . forgive me . . . I just couldn't hold it back any more.

SLOANE I can't pull any punches with you. This is deadly serious . . . maybe even fatal.

43

DENNIS It was my fault, leaving that damned letter around.

SLOANE It doesn't matter whose fault it is. It happened! That's all that counts. One moment of panic may have destroyed our whole case . . .

ANITA But I didn't sign anything.

SLOANE I know!

ANITA He said, "Tell Dennis, if he drops the lawsuit and promises never to write about me, I won't write about him, ever again." That's what we want, isn't it? If all this stops, we can live normal lives again.

SLOANE Can you? Anita, a lie lives as long as the last person who heard it. There was only one way to "finish" it: Stamp it out, lie by lie.

ANITA You make it sound too late now.

DENNIS Bob—are you saying you want to pull out of this case?

SLOANE Go home, both of you. I'll call you later.

ANITA Bob . . .

SLOANE Please, Anita. Go home!

DENNIS Let's go, darling.
        (DENNIS *takes* ANITA *and they start to exit*)

DENNIS It's my fault. I should have told you about the letter . . . prepared you for it.
        (*They exit.* BALDWIN *shuts the door*)

BALDWIN (*To* COLES) All right, Ab—now do you think I "have a right"?

COLES (*Pleading*) Jim, please . . .

BALDWIN (*To* SLOANE) Damn it, we're either partners or we're not. (*Putting down a letter on the desk.* SLOANE *reacts, puzzled*) Standard's letter . . . they're asking for a substitution of attorneys at once . . . and not just on the appeal . . . (SLOANE, *stunned, picks up the letter*) She's given you a way out. Take it! I'll get on the phone and call Mercer at Standard.

SLOANE Jim, wait . . .

BALDWIN It's a hundred-and-twenty-five-thousand-dollar-a-year retainer!

SLOANE I know!

BALDWIN Bob, at best this wasn't the strongest case in the world. And who needs moral victories at *this* stage of the game?!

SLOANE (*Turning on him suddenly*) Damn it, *I* do! That's who! If he's allowed to silence Corcoran today, tomorrow it's somebody else. And the day after, the whole country. *I* can't let it happen! Don't you understand that?!

BALDWIN (*Exasperated but controlled*) What do you want me to do about this?

SLOANE Acknowledge it with our usual regrets. Please, Jim?

Curtain

45

Act Two

The scene is a courtroom of the New York State Supreme Court. There is the judge's bench, counsel table, the principal parties and the witnesses. The trial is in progress. We see the JUDGE. SLOANE, COLES, DENNIS, *and* DAVID *are at one side of counsel table.* CLEARY, BENDIX, CLEARY'S ASSISTANT *are at the other side. The* COURT STENOGRAPHER *is in his place and taking notes. The* COURT CLERK *sits below the judge's bench.*

SLOANE   And now, Dennis, would you trace for us, briefly, your career as a war correspondent, for the ten years *after* that?

DENNIS   I stayed in Europe for the most part, covering the invasion of Poland, the Battle of France, the Battle of Britain, all the while trying to wake up the rest of the world to the Nazi danger.

SLOANE   The defendants printed certain statements reflecting on your actions, motivations, and courage during the late war . . . Dennis, I ask you now if any of them are true?

CLEARY *(Interrupting)*   Your Honor, are we to be treated to the spectacle of a witness *and* a party to this lawsuit being asked to evaluate his own courage?

JUDGE   Surely, Mr. Sloane, you don't intend to ask such a question, do you?

49

SLOANE   I *had* thought a simple question might save the time of the court, but if Mr. Cleary insists I will take a slower, more tedious route . . . During the days before the outbreak of the war when the Nazis were tyrannizing Germany, where were you?

DENNIS   In Germany.

SLOANE   And when France fell so tragically before Hitler's *panzer* divisions, where were you?

DENNIS   In France.

SLOANE   And when the deadly Battle of Britain was on and the Luftwaffe bombed London night after night, where were you?

DENNIS   In London.

SLOANE   And were you in these places by chance or choice?

CLEARY   I object.

JUDGE   Sustained.

SLOANE   One more question, then. Dennis, did you happen to run across Mr. Bendix in any of these places?

CLEARY   I object! Your Honor, this is completely immaterial!

SLOANE   (*Using the moment to make a point to the jury*) Your Honor, if I had asked if Mr. Bendix was there, I would have anticipated an objection from Mr. Cleary. Or even if I had asked . . . where *was* Mr. Bendix during all these times of danger, Mr. Cleary might well have objected. But all I did was ask my own client whom he happened to meet, or *not* meet, during certain *interesting* and *dangerous* days in his life. Does Your Honor deem such a question objectionable?

JUDGE (*Secretly amused*)   If Mr. Cleary wishes to renew his objection . . .

CLEARY   And bring forth another of Mr. Sloane's "helpful" and "enlightening" explanations? Allow the question!

SLOANE   Dennis?

DENNIS   No, I did not meet Ben . . . I mean Mr. Bendix . . . in any of those places.
(SLOANE *and* CLEARY *both react to this slip*)

SLOANE   Now, Dennis, I ask you, have you ever been a member of any group, party or organization which is hostile to or aimed at overthrowing the Government of the United States?

DENNIS   No, sir.

SLOANE   Have you ever knowingly taken any step or action hostile to or disloyal to this Government?

DENNIS   Never!

SLOANE   Thank you, Dennis. That is all.
(CLEARY *rising and advancing toward* DENNIS)

CLEARY   Tell me, Mr. Corcoran, did Mr. Sloane ever advise you *not* to refer to Mr. Bendix in this courtroom as "Ben"?

DENNIS   Well, he . . . yes, he did.

CLEARY   Is that why only a moment ago you referred to him as "Ben" and then changed it suddenly to "Mr. Bendix"?

DENNIS   We had been friends long ago . . . and it was a habit that hung over.

CLEARY   And Mr. Sloane thought it might create a wrong impression with the jury?

DENNIS   Yes . . .

CLEARY   Now then, as long as your friendship with Ben— Mr. Bendix—has come up, tell me this: Didn't the first real *open* break in the friendship between you and Ben come about when you wrote an article about him?

DENNIS   I reviewed a book written *about* Mr. Bendix.

CLEARY   Did you agree with the book's appraisal of Mr. Bendix?

DENNIS   In the main, yes.

CLEARY   And you expressed your opinion and said so.

DENNIS   That's what I was asked to do and I did it.

CLEARY   Would you say that was the responsibility as well as the privilege of a newspaperman?

DENNIS   (*Realizing he's blundered into a trap*)   Well, I . . . yes, I would say so.

CLEARY   Available even to those newspapermen with whom we have political differences?

DENNIS   Available to *every* newspaperman who uses it *responsibly* and *honestly*.

CLEARY   As long as *you* are the judge of what is responsible and honest, is that it?

SLOANE   I object to that remark, Your Honor!

JUDGE   Sustained.

CLEARY   Mr. Corcoran, I show you now a copy of a book entitled *Hangman on Horseback* and ask you if this is the volume which you reviewed.

DENNIS *(Takes the book, examines it)*   It is.

CLEARY *(Reaching for the clipping his ASSISTANT hands him)*   Mr. Corcoran, I read to you now from your review titled "Knight with a Twisted Lance." "The old American political saw, 'I'd rather be right than President' has now been superseded by another, 'I'd rather be *far* to the right than anything.' This could well serve as the credo of Boyd Bendix, who is the subject of a crisp crackling biographical analysis by Edwin Curry. Have a sample of this bit of Curried Bendix: 'Bendix is a prime example of the once-great newspaperman who has become so enchanted with his own opinions that he will distort any fact to suit his purpose.' And this: 'Bendix believes in one God and one Country, provided both believe in Boyd Bendix!'" Have I quoted your review correctly?

DENNIS   Yes . . . yes, sir.

CLEARY   And are these your words, Mr. Corcoran? "The author of *Hangman on Horseback* must know Boyd Bendix well, nay, intimately, to know his character so well."

DENNIS   Yes.

53

CLEARY   Now, Mr. Corcoran, do you still insist that your review was fair to Mr. Bendix?

DENNIS   Not only fair, but in its way, favorable.

CLEARY   I must confess your logic escapes *me*. How, favorable?

DENNIS   Because I left *out* more than a hundred and twenty-seven other unfavorable statements about Mr. Bendix, which I would like to read into the record now.

CLEARY   Your Honor, this is preposterous!

JUDGE   Mr. Cleary, *you* opened the door to this testimony by your question. Mr. Corcoran!
(DAVID *hands* DENNIS *the place-marked book*)

DENNIS   To save the jury's time, this one should be enough. Quote. No one has developed the art of self-righteous indignation to a higher degree than Boyd Bendix. And he would be comic if history did not present us with bloody reminders that the extremist with conviction, wrong though he may be, can affect the lives of millions of innocent people. Bendix polishes his words like the knights of old polished their armor. His lance is sharp and skillfully used. Oh, if it were not so red with innocent blood. Unquote.

CLEARY (*At once and sharply*)   Mr. Corcoran, were you in favor of a second front?

DENNIS   For a time.

CLEARY   And was the so-called second front specifically designed to take the pressure off the Reds on the Eastern

Front and place it on American, British and Allied troops on the Western Front?

DENNIS It was designed to win the war!

CLEARY For whom?

DENNIS The Russians were our allies at the time. If we won, we *all* won.

CLEARY Did you know the estimated cost in lives that might be involved? American lives . . .?

DENNIS American lives . . . and others.

CLEARY Yet you seriously *asked, urged, wrote for, argued* for a second front?

DENNIS At that time, yes.

CLEARY And "that time" was the *same* time the Communists were urging it?

DENNIS They always urged a second front. But then I . . . had meetings with the American Supreme Commander —General Eisenhower—and others . . . and they explained the reasons why it would be too dangerous at that time. Once I knew that, I wrote another article reversing my stand and arguing against a second front. Even though the Communists were still in favor of it. I'm not a Communist, I never have been, officially, or in any other way, and I won't let you draw such an inference!

CLEARY Now, sir, the time when you advocated a second front: was that *after* you had been to Moscow to observe that Communist city under attack?

55

DENNIS Yes . . .

CLEARY Thank you. (*He turns away. He is slow, deliberate. Then he turns back*) Oh, before we leave the subject of Moscow, *and* second fronts *and* Communism, did you, when you were in Moscow, happen to meet the defendant, Boyd Bendix, *there*?

DENNIS No, sir.

CLEARY Thank you. Mr. Corcoran, on D-Day, what beach did you land on?

DENNIS No beach. On D-Day . . . I was in Chicago. You see . . .

CLEARY (*Interrupting*) Thank you, Mr. Corcoran.

DENNIS (*Pushing right on*) I had been called back by the Government, so naturally I came.

CLEARY To make public appearances and lectures at several thousand dollars apiece? Almost five thousand miles from the scene of an invasion *you* called for and where American boys were dying on the beaches!

SLOANE I object!

JUDGE Sustained!

CLEARY Would you estimate for us how much you did earn during that time?

DENNIS Well, I . . .

CLEARY Come, come, Mr. Corcoran, surely you can give us an estimate—a guess.

DENNIS Well, five, maybe as much as six thousand dollars . . .

CLEARY A week?

DENNIS Yes, sir.

CLEARY And this was during the invasion of France, the Battle of the Bulge . . .?

SLOANE Your Honor!

CLEARY I withdraw the question.

DENNIS I said I was . . .

CLEARY And I am finished with the witness.
  (CLEARY *turns away and* DENNIS, *knowing he's been had and the effect on the jury is bad, instead of leaving the chair, suddenly explodes*)

DENNIS Well, I'm not finished! You have no right to twist the truth! No right to destroy a man's life with your damned insinuations, your lies!
  (*The* JUDGE *bangs his gavel, as the lights dim*)

Blackout

Several days later. Standing in the witness place, arm upraised, since he is just finishing taking the oath, is a distinguished British officer in uniform. When first we see him he is lowering his arm and being seated and being asked by the CLERK.

CLERK   Your name?

DOUGLAS *(With a slight Scottish burr)*   Douglas, sir.

CLERK   Full name.

DOUGLAS   Evelyn Bruce Robert Mitchell Ian Douglas.

CLERK   Thank you, sir.

STENOGRAPHER   Sorry, Your Honor, I didn't get that. How does he spell his first name?

DOUGLAS   E-v-e-l-y-n.

STENOGRAPHER *(Himself a native of the Bronx)*   Oh, Evuhlyn! H'mm!

SLOANE *(Taking over for direct examination)*   Your rank, sir?

DOUGLAS   Colonel in the Highland Greys Regiment, sir.

SLOANE   And your work during the war?

DOUGLAS   Mainly to escort correspondents to the most active fronts to observe whatever they wanted to see.

SLOANE (*Turning to the table and picking up a photo*) Sir, I show you a photograph and ask were you present when it was taken?

DOUGLAS (*Takes it, looks at it*) Yes, sir. The desert just before El Alamein. The two men *on* the tank are both Aussie privates. The man leaning against the tank is myself. The man with the covering over his head is Dennis Corcoran.

SLOANE I offer this photograph in evidence.

JUDGE Mr. Cleary? (*He waves his lack of protest*) It will be accepted and marked.

SLOANE You said that Mr. Corcoran has a covering over his head?

DOUGLAS His extreme sensitivity to the sun made him go round that way. It amused the men. They called him "a bloody A-rab."

SLOANE How many days were you in this area in the company of the plaintiff?

DOUGLAS Seventeen. I remember him saying, "Seventeen days and no dispatch, my editor'll be sure I've had it." So, against military advice, he insisted on trying to slip through the lines at night and make his way to the Coast to Sfax, then British-held, so he could send his stuff.

SLOANE And did he go?

DOUGLAS Yes, sir. He and I and one other man.

SLOANE Would you tell us what happened as nearly as you can remember it?

DOUGLAS It was the second night. As we were darting from one burned-out tank to another for cover, we must have been spotted, because a German scout plane appeared overhead and dropped flares. We made it into a slit trench and lay there. They started lobbing shells in. They were rather precise because the shells were bursting all around us with disquieting frequency, and proximity, most of the night.

SLOANE And when was it over?

DOUGLAS We started to climb slowly out of the trench and I noticed that Denny's leg was bleeding. He'd been hit by a shell splinter.

SLOANE He'd been wounded. That was the first time you knew it?

DOUGLAS Yes, sir. I bandaged his knee. Then we set out and made it to Sfax two nights later and he filed his story.

SLOANE Now, sir, I ask if you had any other experience with Dennis Corcoran under fire during the last war?

DOUGLAS Yes, sir, the raid on Dieppe.

SLOANE You were there too?

DOUGLAS That was Denny's fault. He started agitating to go along once he got wind of a mission of great importance being planned.

SLOANE Why was Dennis Corcoran, an American, sent to cover a Canadian operation?

DOUGLAS He volunteered. No, *insisted* is the right word. He'd been turned down once.

SLOANE What happened to reverse that?

DOUGLAS He pulled strings, sir.

SLOANE Exactly how?

DOUGLAS He had received a letter from . . .

CLEARY I object, sir. The witness is now testifying to events of which he could not have had first-hand knowledge?

JUDGE Mr. Sloane?

SLOANE If Mr. Cleary insists, we will offer the letter itself in evidence.
(DAVID *is ready with the letter, which* SLOANE *takes and starts to show to* DOUGLAS)

CLEARY I demand to see that letter first, Your Honor.

SLOANE Of course.
(*Gives it to* CLEARY, *who takes it, looks at it*)

CLEARY Your Honor, the authenticity of this letter not having been established, I object to its being received in evidence!

JUDGE Mr. Sloane?

SLOANE Colonel, I show you this letter and ask you, have you seen this signature before?

DOUGLAS More than several hundred times.

SLOANE   Is this, in your opinion, an authentic signature?

DOUGLAS   It is, sir.

SLOANE   Your Honor?

JUDGE   Accepted.

SLOANE   And now would you be kind enough to read the contents of the letter?

CLEARY   Your Honor . . .

JUDGE   Overruled! Proceed, Colonel!

DOUGLAS   "Dennis Corcoran, Connaught Hotel, London. My Dear Sir: I should like you to know how admirable I thought your article last Sunday. I know that your words have given real pleasure and encouragement not only to me, but to a great many people in this island."

SLOANE   And the signature?

DOUGLAS   "Yours faithfully, Winston Churchill."
(CLEARY *makes a sarcastic V-for-victory sign*)

SLOANE   Now will you tell us how this letter came to be delivered into Corcoran's hands?

DOUGLAS   I'd been asked to deliver it and I did. At the same time I brought word that his request to cover the Dieppe raid was turned down.

SLOANE   What happened then?

DOUGLAS   He sat down and wrote a note to Sir Winston saying, "My Dear Sir, If you would like to give real pleasure and encouragement to just one *more* person on this island, give him a chance to get the hell off it and go on that secret mission. Yours faithfully, Dennis Corcoran."

SLOANE   And what was the Prime Minister's reaction to that?

DOUGLAS   He sent Mr. Corcoran his approval. And a case of whiskey. (*There is laughter. In all seriousness*) There is no higher commendation from Sir Winston.

SLOANE   Do you know what happened to that case of Scotch whiskey?

CLEARY   Your Honor, could that case be relevant to the case here on trial . . .

JUDGE   Perhaps not. But the court has a judicial curiosity about that whiskey.

DOUGLAS   When I arrived, Denny's room was full of Yank fliers who were attached to the RAF. It was always open house for those lads at Denny's place.

SLOANE   That day, sir . . .

DOUGLAS   Well, I entered with the case of whiskey. *And* the letter of permission, of course. Denny was elated. He ripped the top off the case . . . handed each Yank a bottle. Then he sent them all down to the bar and phoned down that everything was to be put on his bill.

SLOANE   Would you say that was strange conduct for a man accused of "profiteering" from the war?

CLEARY   Object!

JUDGE Sustained!

SLOANE Now, sir, several days after that you both embarked for the Dieppe raid?

DOUGLAS Yes, sir.

SLOANE Will you describe that raid, as briefly as you can, sir?

DOUGLAS Well, it was an exploratory mission, prior to the invasion. The purpose was to get in close to Dieppe, land troops, hold the city for some eight hours and effect certain vital damage and then withdraw with a minimum loss of lives and casualties.

SLOANE And how did the mission go, sir?

DOUGLAS It's well known, it was a great disaster.

SLOANE Was *your* ship under attack?

DOUGLAS *Heavy* attack, sir.

SLOANE And did Denny remain on deck during the entire battle?

DOUGLAS Except when he was carrying the wounded below to be treated.

SLOANE Would you say he performed his function under fire with the zeal, devotion and courage expected of a war correspondent?

DOUGLAS I would say he far *exceeded* the expected zeal, devotion and courage at all times.

64

SLOANE Thank you, sir. Your witness.
(SLOANE *retires,* CLEARY *takes over*)

CLEARY Colonel Douglas . . . I trust that you understand that nothing I ask is intended to reflect discredit on you, your uniform or your people, who have a glorious tradition of courage under fire, most particularly in the Battle of Britain.

SLOANE Your Honor, if Mr. Cleary is now going to raise his glass and toast Her Majesty I think we should *all* be allowed to join.

CLEARY (*He shrugs pleasantly, he's served his purpose of lightening a situation which will get rough*) Sir, is it fair to say that after France fell, your country was in a desperate situation . . .?

DOUGLAS Desperate is a modest word for it.

CLEARY So someone like Dennis Corcoran, who could mobilize sympathy for your plight, was extremely important in influencing us to send you lend-lease supplies and volunteers.

DOUGLAS We were grateful to him *then* and we *still* are! But if you're suggesting that I've come here for any purpose other than to tell the truth, sir, you are mistaken!

CLEARY Colonel . . . is the expression "judas goat" known to you?

DOUGLAS Aye—we, too, have the same expression.

CLEARY Then you know it is used for an animal, be it goat, ram, bull, which leads others of its kind into the slaughterhouse. But at the last moment, the judas goat is shunted through one gate to safety while all the others continue to their death.

DOUGLAS I'm grateful to you for the explanation but it was quite unnecessary.

CLEARY Were not the activities of Dennis Corcoran very much akin to that of a judas goat?

SLOANE Your Honor, I object strenuously to a figure of speech which is, in a way, even more libelous than the libels here on trial!

JUDGE Surely, Mr. Cleary, you can find some suitable language.

CLEARY (*To* DOUGLAS) Sir, is it not true that one of the chief instruments in preparing American public opinion for sending aid to Britain and eventually joining in the war with Britain was Dennis Corcoran?

DOUGLAS As I remember it, the United States entered the war when it was attacked at Pearl Harbor.

CLEARY Which would account for our going to war against the Japanese. Now, as to the second front of which we've heard much in this trial. Would you say that "Denny," did much to stir up fervor for it and then was shunted aside to safety here at home while thousands of *other* Americans plunged into the slaughterhouse that was Omaha Beach?

SLOANE I object!

JUDGE Strike the question. Counselor, you may continue. But within the limits of good taste.

CLEARY Now, Colonel, you testified about certain adventures with Denny. One of them being in the desert. Did I understand correctly that the battle of El Alamein was raging at the time?

DOUGLAS Yes, sir.

CLEARY And during the battle it was so important for Denny to send his story that three men risked their lives to go through the enemy lines?

DOUGLAS I think any conscientious journalist will do his utmost to see that his material gets into print, sir. And has a right to.

CLEARY I didn't hear that last, sir?

DOUGLAS I said, any journalist has a right to see that his material gets into print.

CLEARY Thank you, sir. And Denny felt that way about his report on El Alamein?

DOUGLAS And history has proved him right, sir. It was the turning point of the desert campaign.

CLEARY (*Smiling*) El Alamein? Or Denny's report? I'm sorry, Your Honor, I was confused. Now, sir, you testified that you were aboard the flagship during the Dieppe adventure . . .

DOUGLAS I was.

CLEARY Then do you know whether any correspondents landed with the commando force?

DOUGLAS Yes, sir. Two Canadian correspondents went in with the troops.

CLEARY Did "good old Denny" land on the Dieppe coast or did he remain on board through the entire operation?

DOUGLAS Having been assigned to the flagship, Denny had no personal choice.

CLEARY So that during the eight hours of the operation, during the time that several thousand Canadians were being massacred on the beach and in the streets of Dieppe, this "brave, fearless knight" of the typewriter was safely aboard with the big brass.

DOUGLAS I object to the use of the word "safely."

CLEARY Your Honor, the witness, being a stranger to our courts, obviously is not aware that the right to object is limited solely to counsel.

JUDGE Sir, Mr. Cleary is right. Answer the question, please.

DOUGLAS I'm sorry, Your Lordship—uh—Your Honor—the mistake *is* mine. From what I had observed, I thought it was only the right to be *objectionable* that was limited to counsel.

(*There is laughter, which the* JUDGE *gavels down*)

CLEARY Colonel . . . didn't you testify, in a rather colorful way, that Denny-boy practically forced Sir Winston to send him on that mission?

DOUGLAS   Sir Winston is always one to make a joke or *take* a joke with considerable zest, sir.

CLEARY   Fine. Now I ask you, as long as Denny was "making such a joke," couldn't he have asked for the assignment that would put him *ashore* at Dieppe and *not* on the most protected vessel in the entire fleet?

DOUGLAS   The flagship, sir, is the nerve center of the operation.

CLEARY   And naturally the most protected.

DOUGLAS   Quite the contrary, sir. With all the special wireless and radar equipment sticking up out of her, she was a marked ship for attack from air and shore batteries. In fact that day—

CLEARY   Did she move into the shore . . .

SLOANE   Allow the witness to finish his answer.

CLEARY   He has finished it!

JUDGE   Mr. Cleary! Now, Colonel, continue.

DOUGLAS   That day we were under continuous attack from the air. And about twenty-five percent of the men aboard the *Calpe* were casualties, half of those dead. One time Denny and I were standing in the observation bridge alongside two junior officers when an ME came in and strafed the deck. Both young men were hit. Denny carried one below to the wardroom. I took the other one. They were using the dining tables for surgery. When Denny put him down the doctor took one look and said, "This lad's dead." Denny nodded and said, "I know. But

69

it didn't seem right to leave him up there." Hours later, we stood on the bridge deck looking down at the destruction. He reached for a cigarette and when he came up with it, it was damp and discolored. The blood of that lad had seeped through Denny's combat uniform. I slipped one of my own cigarettes into his lips, lit it and he began to draw on it, deep draws, never taking it from his lips, till it burned down so far I had to brush it away so he wouldn't burn himself. There is something holy about a last contact between two human beings. Dennis Corcoran felt it that day.

CLEARY (*Not daring to attack now*)   That will be all, sir.
   (DOUGLAS *starts to rise but stops, which causes the* JUDGE *to ask*)

JUDGE   Is there something you wish to add?

DOUGLAS   It strikes me now, Your Lordship, that I never did quite answer the question. About the relative safety of a flagship . . . anyone who'd seen them hosing the blood off the decks of the *Calpe* that evening wouldn't need to ask the question . . .
   (*He begins to leave the stand*)

Blackout

Scene 3

One week later. The lights come up on SLOANE *as the* JUDGE *is responding to his request.*

JUDGE   Mr. Sloane, you have had many months to prepare your case. The witness you refer to has been in the jurisdiction and subject to subpoena all that time. Hence, the court does not feel justified in allowing you to close your case now subject to re-opening later to present yet another witness . . . especially since you cannot even now guarantee his appearance.

SLOANE   Your Honor, this particular witness, Frederick Alston, is vital to our case, else I would not even make this request.

JUDGE   If Mr. Cleary has no objection . . .

CLEARY (*Knowing that* SLOANE'S *witness will never materialize he can be gracious*)   Your Honor, out of respect to Mr. Sloane's plight, which from time to time befalls all mortal lawyers, we will interpose no objection to Mr. Sloane's presenting the Witness Alston *whenever* he is available.

JUDGE   Very well, I will give you twenty-four hours to produce the witness.

SLOANE   Thank you, Your Honor . . . Thank you, Mr. Cleary.

JUDGE Now, Mr. Cleary, the defendant's case, if you will.

CLEARY Your Honor, Mr. Boyd Bendix will be our first witness!

CLERK Mr. Boyd Bendix. (BENDIX *comes forward to take the stand. The* CLERK *administers the oath*) Do you solemnly swear that the testimony you are about to give is the truth and the whole truth, so help you God?

BENDIX So help me God!
(*He remains standing*)

JUDGE Be seated, Mr. Bendix.

CLEARY If Your Honor please, there being no specific rule against it, I ask the court to allow Mr. Bendix to stand while testifying.

JUDGE If Mr. Sloane has no particular objection . . . the court has none.

SLOANE We so welcome the sight of Mr. Bendix in the witness box that we'll take him any way we can get him, sitting, standing or lying down!

CLEARY (*Smiling*) Thank you. Now, sir, your name?

BENDIX Boyd Bendix, the Second.

CLEARY Your profession?

BENDIX Journalist, columnist, writer of the truth as I see it.

CLEARY Is it a fact, sir, that you have been honored with a Pulitzer Prize, the highest award that American journalism can bestow on one of its own?

BENDIX Yes, sir.

CLEARY Mr. Bendix, can you tell us what is your personal creed as a newspaperman?

BENDIX To expose to the American people its enemies, whether they are on the right or the left, in Big Labor or in Big Business, in Government or out.

CLEARY Would you consider immorality un-American?

BENDIX Anything that destroys the fiber of the individual American eventually destroys America. Drunkenness, lechery, contamination of the races are all forces of destruction of this country.

CLEARY So that when you write against these things you do so out of duty?

BENDIX Yes, sir.

CLEARY And in writing the articles complained of by the plaintiff, you were not concerned so much with writing *about* Dennis Corcoran as with *informing* the American public about certain evils?

BENDIX My object was to inform the American people of the truth about Corcoran, his fellow-traveling friends who were bleeding this country white with one hand, while painting it red with the other.

CLEARY Now, sir, how did you go about gathering the facts on Mr. Corcoran?

BENDIX Research. Endless reading and collecting of articles, references and items concerning Mr. Corcoran in the public press for many years.

SLOANE   Here it comes! Section Three Thirty-eight in all its gory glory!

CLEARY (*With a glance at* SLOANE, *then to* BENDIX)   Since I do not wish to tax the jury with "endless" articles I am going to show you a mere handful and I ask you if these are taken from your files and constitute part of the material on which you relied in writing your articles about Mr. Corcoran.

SLOANE   I ask the court to instruct the jury . . . *each time* Mr. Cleary puts such a piece of trash into evidence . . . that its admission under Section Three Thirty-eight is not an endorsement of its truth . . . but that it is being admitted *only* in an attempt to minimize damages.

JUDGE   Mr. Sloane, Section Three Thirty-eight states very clearly that such evidence, true or false, can be introduced by defendant provided he relied on such evidence in writing his own articles. Continue, Mr. Cleary.

CLEARY (*To* BENDIX)   Now, sir, I show you this clipping and ask you to read the words underlined in it.

BENDIX (*Taking the clipping*)   "The true shame of it is that Dennis Corcoran, who has received the best that a free America has to offer, position, success, acclaim, should take now the Red Road to Russian Communism."

CLEARY   The source, sir?

BENDIX   The magazine *The Word*. A monthly religious publication from Boston.

CLEARY   And did you *rely* on that statement when writing your articles about Corcoran?

BENDIX   Yes, sir.

SLOANE   Your Honor?

JUDGE (*To the jury*)   Ladies and gentlemen, the fact that this is allowed in evidence does not vouch for its truth but merely indicates that Mr. Bendix used it as a source for his articles about Mr. Corcoran and as such is to be considered by you in determining if he acted recklessly and carelessly in writing his articles.

SLOANE   And as to cross-examination, Your Honor?

JUDGE   And, of course, as you can see, since this is nothing more than a clipping, Mr. Sloane is deprived of the right to cross-examine, as he would do if a witness were testifying in these same words.

SLOANE   Thank you, Your Honor.

CLEARY   And now, sir, *this* clipping from your files . . .

BENDIX   The *Voice of Freedom,* Topeka, Kansas. The date January eleventh, 1951. "It is a small coterie of disciples clustered around that prophet of Sin, Eliot Andrews, who tell this country what to think and believe. Steeped in sin, bloated from excess of food and wine, given to lechery of every sort, including the mating of white and black. And chief among his disciples is the notorious foreign correspondent, Dennis Corcoran, who apes his mentor in every evil way."

CLEARY   And did you, sir, accept this as true and rely on it in writing about the plaintiff?

BENDIX   Yes, sir.

SLOANE   Your Honor ...

JUDGE   The same instruction prevails.

SLOANE   I ask that the instruction be repeated in detail. Or shall we assume that the jury can hear this with one half their minds for one purpose and disregard it with the other half? These articles are false! I insist that be pointed out!

JUDGE (*Gaveling*)   Mr. Sloane! Mr. Sloane!

SLOANE   I'm sorry, Your Honor, but we are dealing here with the heart of this case!

JUDGE   Mr. Sloane, unless and until the State Legislature repeals Section Three Thirty-eight the statute is clear. The jury has already been cautioned once. This case will proceed!

CLEARY   Now, sir, since Mr. Sloane is so insistent, do you have any first-hand evidence supporting the article you just read?

BENDIX   Yes, sir. One sunny Sunday afternoon, Mr. Corcoran and a certain young lady . . . showed up at our house, in a state of almost complete nudity. He in bathing trunks, and she in . . . brief bathing shorts and . . . a top . . . though the brevity of it and the jaunty angle at which it was worn made no secret of her . . . her glandular endowments, which were, to say the least, impressive. Both she and Corcoran were under the influence of liquor. And they demanded that we allow them to come into the house and take a shower. But when they made it clear they intended to take a shower *together,* my wife insisted that they leave our house, which they did. However, on the lawn before our house there is a fish pond. And this man, sir, seizing that girl's hand, suddenly plunged into that pond. And there followed a scene of . . . of, well, let me only say, unspeakable vulgarity. Though not unexpected after what Mrs. Eliot Andrews herself said about him. Mrs. Andrews told me—

SLOANE   I object to this as being hearsay evidence!

CLEARY   It would be hearsay, if we were introducing it for any other purpose. But quite admissible under Section Three Thirty-eight as reliance testimony.

JUDGE   Overruled.

SLOANE   Then I ask Your Honor to instruct the jury that whatever this is, it is not being admitted as to truth.

JUDGE   The jury understands that, I'm sure. But your objection is noted.

CLEARY   Now, sir, the incident which was related to you by Mrs. Andrews . . .

BENDIX   Mrs. Andrews told me that one sunny day in late summer when she was boating out on the lake on their property . . . Corcoran suddenly came up into view, evidently having swum toward the boat under water to surprise her. Then he took hold of the gunnels and lifted himself into the boat to sit opposite her, stark naked.

CLEARY   You said "stark naked"?

BENDIX   Not I said, *she* said. And she went on to say, "He climbed into the boat, without so much as a hairnet on.

77

He sat there in the boat facing me and with his lavaliere dangling."
(*The crowd reacts, shocked. The* JUDGE *gavels the courtroom to silence*)

JUDGE   This trial will proceed in an orderly fashion or else it will proceed behind closed doors! Mr. Cleary . . .

CLEARY   Are you sure, sir, that those were the exact words used by Mrs. Andrews?

BENDIX   One is not apt to forget such a phrase.

CLEARY   Now, sir, I ask you, in view of the events of many, many months that have passed since you wrote that first article about Dennis Corcoran concerning his cowardice, debauchery, drunkenness, lewdness and leftish leanings, would you now retract one word of it?

BENDIX   It is my duty as a newspaperman in the exercise of a free press to make public such facts. I withdraw nothing!

CLEARY   Thank you, Mr. Bendix.

JUDGE   The court will adjourn until tomorrow at ten A.M. You are excused, Mr. Bendix.
(*They all rise*)

Blackout

The lights come down and go up on the office of ROBERT
SLOANE; *it is late the same night.* SLOANE, DENNIS, ANITA
and COLES *are there.* DAVID *appears in the doorway.*

SLOANE   Well?

DAVID   The night elevator man says that he brought no
one up to this floor since the dinner arrived.

SLOANE   Thanks, David. (DAVID *exits*) There it is, Denny.
Your "friend" Fred Alston.

DENNIS   He promised *this* time he'd show up!

SLOANE   And I've been going on that basis for months. Yet
here we are, our case is finished and without Alston it's
not good enough. (ANITA *sits up, her move a question.*
SLOANE *might as well start preparing them for the truth
now*) A few effective witnesses don't prove a case or win
a suit! Sure, all our witnesses have been good. But God
Himself could come into court and testify to your courage and character and we could still lose. Damage! Damage, man! That's what we have to prove. And Alston is
the key to that.

ANITA   The canceled speech. We have proof of that!

SLOANE   One speech . . . a few thousand dollars . . . I
wouldn't depend on that too much.

COLES   Or even on malice, in a case like *this.*

79

DENNIS   What do you mean?

COLES   In a case where you can't prove damages, the jury can award you a substantial verdict sometimes, if you can prove that the defendant deliberately, maliciously or recklessly set out to hurt you.

DENNIS   What did you mean by "a case like *this*"?
(COLES *looks to* SLOANE. *They have obviously had discussions about it and* SLOANE *decides to explain, reluctantly*)

SLOANE   Denny, when you try a case, it isn't all law. Or even witnesses. There's the emotional climate that surrounds the case. And it's running against us. Strongly.

ANITA   If the jury believes our witnesses, how can you say that?

SLOANE   Nita, there are words that have special meanings, built-in, pre-conditioned meanings . . . mother, God, Fourth of July, apple pie, coffee . . . words to which almost everyone will react with warmth, with friendliness . . . then there are *other* words, words that haunt, terrorize.

ANITA   Communism . . .

SLOANE   The dirtiest word in the dictionary. (*To* DENNIS) Right now, you're on trial for being part of a Communist strategy to use American boys to save Russian lives! That's the issue! Face it! (*Moving to his desk to get sheaf of testimony*) It's in here. In Cleary's cross-examination of you. In Bendix's testimony. And all it takes is for *one* juror to be infected by the virus and we're through! There are people in this country using words like "traitor" now about Roosevelt, about General Marshall, about the Chief Justice of the United States. Do you realize the danger *you're* in? So we need proof of damages. Not just for legal reasons, but emotional ones as well. We have to prove Bendix is choking you to death economically. That's why without Alston our case isn't strong enough. Legally *or* emotionally. Not anywhere near strong enough.

(SLOANE *turns away and* DENNIS *misinterprets his move*)

DENNIS   I'm sorry . . . sorry I ever got you involved.

SLOANE (*Turning on him*)   Dennis, let's get one thing straight, win or lose . . . I got myself involved! Right, Ab?

COLES   Right.

SLOANE   And if the case isn't as strong as I'd like, don't start conceding any elections yet! Get on that phone, call Alston again!

(DENNIS *moves to the phone, starts to dial*)

ANITA   Remind him of that day he promised he'd do everything he could to help!

DENNIS (*Nodding till he interrupts with a gesture meaning "I've got an answer"*)   Fred Alston, please. (*Pause*) Keep ringing! I'll hold. (*Pause*) Maybe if you tried the Editorial Board room . . . please! (*Pause*) Hello, Fred? Gone for the night? How long ago did he leave? Two

81

hours? When I called the last time, they said . . . well,
never mind . . . thanks. Yeah, thanks.
(*He hangs up*)

COLES Now you know why we didn't subpoena him. A
witness like that, you want *voluntarily* . . . or *not at all.*

DENNIS He promised! He told me only this morning . . . I
tell you, he'll *be* here!

SLOANE All right, we'll give him till (*Consulting his
watch*) till midnight. Now, let's get back to Bendix's
testimony. (*Moving to the desk to get the testimony
which* COLES *hands to him*) That story he told about
Mrs. Andrews and the boat . . .

DENNIS I swear to God, Bob, nothing like that ever happened!

ANITA (*When* SLOANE *doesn't answer*) Don't you believe
him?

SLOANE It's not that. I almost wish it *had* happened. With
a story that is partly true, at least you have something to
work with . . . a fact here, a detail there, that you can
use to trip up the witness. But with a complete fabrica-
tion, and Mrs. Andrews dead, it's simply your word
against Bendix. And he's a pretty convincing witness.

DENNIS It just never happened!

SLOANE But how do we prove that?
(DAVID *comes in with a fresh pot of coffee and pours
it*)

82

SLOANE (*Acknowledging the fresh coffee*) Thanks, David. Anita! Did you ever hear a *woman* use the expression "he wasn't even wearing a hairnet" to indicate nudity?

ANITA No.

SLOANE Sounded strange to me, too, for a woman . . .

DAVID But he had it written down!

SLOANE (*Turning to* DAVID) *Who* had it written down?

DAVID I . . . I'm very good at reading upside down. In fact . . .

COLES . . . "he reads better upside down than most people do right side up."

SLOANE *Who* had *what* written down?

DAVID When I was passing their counsel table, I glanced down and noticed that before Bendix left to take the stand he had written down the words "without even a fig leaf" and then crossed them out. And below them the words "without even a hairnet on."

SLOANE (*Taking hold of* DAVID, *sitting him down*) You saw that, you're sure?

DAVID Positive. But the word that had me puzzled was "lavaliere." That's such an unusual word that upside down it hardly seems like any word at all. You see, first he had written down and crossed out . . .
　　(*Embarrassed, he stops*)

SLOANE What?

83

A CASE OF LIBEL

DAVID (*Sheepishly in* ANITA's *presence*) He had written down and crossed out "sat there with his three-piece set showing."

DENNIS Leave it to Ben to come up with a phrase like that—

SLOANE (*Intent on following his own thought, he waves* DENNIS *quiet, concentrates on finishing with* DAVID) But he crossed that out . . . and *then* had written down . . .

DAVID Just the word "lavaliere," which I didn't recognize at all till he actually used it on the stand.

SLOANE (*He's made a big discovery*) Well, thank *you.* Thank you very, very *much.*

COLES I think this boy really did study hanging from a trapeze.

SLOANE Well, that's okay with me. Because finally I know what Bendix strategy is! That's Bendix language, selected very carefully to make an impression on the jury. And to make it *stick!* (*Suddenly*) David . . . that piece of paper. What did it look like? (*Impatiently*) The one Bendix was writing on!

DAVID The usual yellow legal. Why?

SLOANE (*Turns to the desk to pick up a pad and pencil*) Wrote like this?
      (*He writes*)

DAVID Yes.

84

SLOANE And then?

DAVID Sir?

SLOANE Did he leave it there. Or did he . . .? (*He rips off a page*) Do this . . . (*He folds it, starts to put it in his pocket*) Or this . . . (*Crumples it*) What did he do with it?

DAVID I . . . I don't remember . . . (SLOANE *turns away handling the ball of paper*) I guess I didn't notice . . . I'm sorry . . .
   (SLOANE *drops the ball of paper onto a prominent place on the desk. As he does, a stranger opens the door from the outer office, looks in cautiously.* SLOANE *turns sharply to look. But* DENNIS *goes to greet him*)

DENNIS Fred! Fred, come on in!

ALSTON (*A hint of liquor on him*) The door was open, the lights were on, so I just . . . well, here I am.

ANITA (*Delighted to see him*) Oh, Fred! Fred! (*She goes to him, kisses him with*) How's Helen? And the kids?

ALSTON Oh, fine. Fine!

DENNIS (*To* SLOANE) I told you he'd show up. Fred . . . this is my lawyer, Mr. Sloane.

ALSTON Sorry I'm late. Stopped for a drink with the boys.

SLOANE (*Shaking hands with him*) I can't tell you how glad I am to see you, Mr. Alston. It's no secret, we need your testimony . . . need it very badly.

ALSTON   How's it been going? The papers don't cover it much.

SLOANE   Gentlemen's agreement. Papers never give much coverage to suits against other papers. Sort of freedom of the press to suppress. Now the key to a case like this is being able to prove the clear simple fact that what the defendant did and said caused the plaintiff to lose opportunity, work, money. That's where you come in.

ALSTON   I'll do whatever I can.
(COLES *brightens for the first time, moves in closer.* DENNIS *and* ANITA *exchange delighted looks. She settles on the couch.* DENNIS *is on the other corner of the couch.* SLOANE *gestures* ALSTON *to a chair and when he is seated,* SLOANE *signals* DAVID *to take notes*)

SLOANE   Let's start with that day you had to turn down Denny's article. We have Denny's version. We have to check yours against it. So I want everything you said and did.

ALSTON (*As though trying to reconstruct*)   Well, I got to the restaurant first. A little early in fact. So I had a drink. And then another one. Then Denny got there and we had one *together* and I got pretty looped. So when I started talking about the manuscript . . . well, I guess whatever Denny told you I said I must have said.

SLOANE   Look, Alston . . . Fred, you can't go into court and say "whatever he said is the truth." Don't you see, we need detailed corroboration of Denny's version.

86

ALSTON   I'll try. But I don't remember precisely.

SLOANE   (*Trying to help him recollect, he acts it out*)   You
were here. Denny here. You reached under your chair,
handed him the envelope . . . then got up and left in a
hurry . . .

ALSTON   (*As though straining to remember*)   I reached
down and . . .? (*To* DENNY) You sure?

DENNIS   Fred, don't you remember . . . you said, "They
can't carry your stuff any more . . . they don't dare . . ."
You remember *that*, don't you ?

ALSTON   Denny, are you sure that I said . . .

DENNIS   Do you think I'll ever forget it? Now, Fred . . .

SLOANE   (*Intervening, lest* DENNIS *lose his control*)   Denny.

DENNIS   Fred, I've seen you drunk before and you remembered the next day. Everything!

SLOANE   Denny! (DENNIS *controls himself and lets* SLOANE
take over) Now, Fred, Denny said that day was different
in at least *one* respect . . .

ALSTON   (*Anticipating and ready*)   Right. It was the first
time we turned down one of his articles . . . but hell,
that happens sooner or later to every writer.

SLOANE   I meant that usually you had your meeting about
rewrites first and *then* went to lunch, correct? (ALSTON
nods) But this particular time, you skipped the meeting
and had lunch first. Why?

ALSTON (*Relieved, he seizes the way out*) Because it was the first time we rejected an article of Denny's.

SLOANE Tell us how you felt about that . . . from the moment you decided you had to turn down Denny's article . . .

ALSTON Well, in the first place, I didn't like it, didn't like it at all. (*Fearing his words might be misinterpreted*) The idea of having to turn down any article of his. (*To* DENNIS) Believe me, Denny! In fact, when Deak first brought it up . . .

SLOANE "Deak"?

ALSTON Deak Tuttle . . . at the Editorial Board meeting . . .

SLOANE So the whole Editorial Board was involved?

ALSTON (*Realizing he may have tipped something, he is quick with a "logical" reason*) You don't think we'd take a step as drastic as this . . . I mean turning down one of Dennis Corcoran's articles without a full meeting of the Board? And believe me (*To* DENNIS) it wasn't unanimous by a long shot. In fact, I was against it. And two other fellows . . . and we said, "It can be saved. With a major rewrite we could stress the American aspect of it and tone down the international aspect . . . give it an 'it affects us here at home' slant" . . . you know there's a sizable percentage of our readership doesn't go for the United Nations and foreign aid and things like that, and while we may not *agree* with them we do have to take them into account . . . so I thought . . . suggested we play down the international aspect and lean on—

88

DENNIS Fred, you never mentioned any of this to me . . .
(SLOANE *grips* DENNIS' *arm, silencing him.* DENNIS
drops back, looks at ANITA, *shocked*)

SLOANE Go on, Alston.

ALSTON And it was right about there that someone—I
don't remember who it was—said maybe Corcoran's out
of step with the times . . . maybe people are fed *up* with
the war and the aftermath of war and talking about the
next war . . . you know, our advertisers are beginning to
kick . . . after all, they're only interested in selling mer-
chandise and it's our job to create an atmosphere in
which they can . . . and believe me, threats don't
help . . . (*The word is out finally and the others onstage
get it.* ALSTON *tries to recoup*) I mean, a woman reading
about threat of a hydrogen war any minute is not likely
to rush out and buy a washing machine that's guaranteed
to last a lifetime, you know? (*He's made a joke and self-
consciously looks to them for the laugh, but it doesn't
come*) I know what you're thinking and you're wrong!
There was no threat from any advertisers mentioned at
that meeting! None! The name Bendix never even came
up! (*Since he was the first to mention this, the others
greet him with silent accusations, pulling back from him
gradually*) I remember that! I wasn't drunk then! When
I talked to *Denny* I was drunk—I don't remember what
I said to him—but I remember what happened at that
meeting! And there was nothing said about letters from
advertisers or readers . . . or anybody being Bendixed . . .
(*When he realizes he has let the words slip that he said
to* DENNIS *that day, he reacts like a caught criminal*)

89

. . . nothing! It was an editorial decision . . . it had nothing to do with . . . look, don't blame me! I had nothing
to do with it—I was against it. And I never wanted to
tell Denny . . . they made me. I said I'm a friend of
his . . . and they said that's exactly why you have to tell
him. And I said I won't even know how to tell him.
And they said you'll find a way. So I slammed out of
there. I went down and took a drink and another and
another and I—Jesus, you don't think I wanted to have
anything to do with it, do you? Do you? (*He is beginning to fall apart*) Now, I don't remember . . . so leave
me alone . . . leave me . . . stop accusing me . . . I just
don't remember!

    (ALSTON *drops into the chair, trembling*)

SLOANE You remember all right. But there's your wife,
the kids, the house in New Canaan, the two cars, the
mortgage. So don't get messed up with anyone who's
controversial, because it might be contagious. I understand all that. But a man's life is involved here. And one
word from you can save him.

ANITA Fred?

COLES (*When it is obvious that* ALSTON *is never going to
answer*) Well, one lie you're not going to get away
with! You didn't come here to chicken out because of
your wife or your kids or anything but one thing, you!

SLOANE Ab!

COLES You coward! A whole world of cowards! Cowards!
    (COLES *starts to tremble and* SLOANE *goes to him, to
    gently move him away.* COLES *turns upstage to re-*

cover. SLOANE *digs into his pocket, takes out some bills and hands them to* DAVID)

SLOANE   Get him a few more drinks. And then make sure he gets on the right train to New Canaan.

DAVID   Yes, sir.
(DAVID *starts out, waiting at the door for* ALSTON, *who picks up his coat, starts to exit but feels compelled to stop*)

ALSTON   Denny, believe me, if I had a choice. I'm not that kind of guy, honest, I'm not.

SLOANE   *Nobody* is. Till the pressure is on.
(DAVID *and* ALSTON *exit.* COLES *breaks the moment of silence that follows*)

COLES   Sorry. But suddenly it all came back. What seemed so far in the past . . .

ANITA   (*Wondering if she understands correctly*)   Ab?

COLES   Yes, I "fought and won."

DENNIS   And "losing is even tougher." Isn't it? Isn't that what you said!

SLOANE   (*Before they can become demoralized he steps in*) Now, wait. So we *can't* prove damages. There's still malice.

DENNIS   Which you'd rather not have to fall back on.

COLES   (*Assembling their assets*)   Bendix's vicious answer to our complaint will help prove malice . . . and getting that speech canceled . . .

DENNIS You said that wasn't enough.

SLOANE It isn't . . . none of it is . . .

ANITA (*Fearfully*) Bob . . .

SLOANE We have to bring it out somehow. It's there. *The malice is in the man.* We have to crack him open and pry it out.

DENNIS You can't crack Ben. I know him better than you do.

SLOANE We don't have any choice.

DENNIS But how? Where do you start on a guy like him?

SLOANE Maybe he's told us that himself. Sex and politics. His two favorite weapons . . . what if we used *them* on *him*?
> (*Moves to the desk, picks up the ball of yellow paper and opens it, then suddenly crumples it again*)

Curtain

Act Three

Scene 1

The courtroom, the next morning. BENDIX *is standing in his place in the witness box.* SLOANE *has begun to cross-examine. The courtroom and the participants are as before, including* DENNIS, ANITA, COLES *and* DAVID.

SLOANE   So, Mr. Bendix, you have been a widely read columnist for News International syndicate for how many years?

BENDIX   Nineteen years.

SLOANE   And in how many newspapers does your column appear?

BENDIX   Eighty-six.

SLOANE   So that you are a man of considerable power . . .

BENDIX   I prefer to say a man of considerable responsibility.

SLOANE   Would you define that responsibility for us?

BENDIX   To bring the truth to the American people. To unmask fraud, lies, deceit, treason . . .

SLOANE   And sin?

BENDIX   And sin! The root of *all* the evils gnawing at the fiber of the American character.

SLOANE   And you have written about this four times a week for nineteen years . . .

95

A CASE OF LIBEL

BENDIX   I have.

SLOANE   There must be a powerful lot of sin around to provide so much for you to write about.

BENDIX   The human race is going to hell in a handbasket if you want the truth of it! America most of all!

SLOANE   Tell me, sir, as a young man, did you ever engage in sexual relationships with young women to whom you were not married?

BENDIX   I had a normal youth.

SLOANE   Which included "wenching about"? (*When* BEN-DIX *does not answer at once*) I hope you don't mind my borrowing a phrase you used about my client. Would you say that in your youth, before you were married, you did your share of wenching about?

BENDIX   I would.

SLOANE   And "nuding about" as well?

BENDIX   No, sir!

SLOANE   Shall we assume then that you wenched about with your clothes *on*?

BENDIX   The phrase "nuding about" which I used in relation to your client concerned appearing in the nude *in public* with a certain nude young woman. If you insist on using my phrases, use them fully and in context.

SLOANE   I shall be extremely careful, sir. Since the jury might be a bit confused by now, shall we summarize?

You did wench about . . . and I assume in the nude . . . but not in public view. Is that correct?

BENDIX (*With some suppressed irritation*)   Yes.

SLOANE (*Taking a photo from among the exhibits*)   Mr. Bendix, I show you Plaintiff's Exhibit Seventeen previously introduced into evidence and ask you to describe it.

BENDIX (*Studying the photograph*)   This seems to be a photograph of some soldiers and an army tank in desert terrain of some kind. A British tank, I think.

SLOANE   Do you recognize the man with the towel on his head?

BENDIX   He . . . he seems to be Dennis Corcoran.

SLOANE   Now I show you this second photograph . . . and ask you to identify it.

BENDIX   It is a photograph of a charity softball game some years back . . . and the people in it are what the public refers to as "celebrities."

SLOANE   Are you in it?

BENDIX   I am captain of the blue team.

SLOANE   Is Mr. Corcoran in it?

BENDIX (*Smiling*)   He is. On the . . . *red* . . . team.

SLOANE   Aside from the color, are you all wearing the *same* uniform?

BENDIX   Yes.

SLOANE   Is it usual for a baseball player to wear a towel sticking out the back of his cap?

BENDIX   No, sir.

SLOANE   Or to wear a dress glove on his throwing hand?

BENDIX   No, sir.

SLOANE   So that in both photographs, taken in daylight, in the sun, he is completely covered?

BENDIX   Practically.

SLOANE   Wearing not less than a hairnet but considerably *more*? (BENDIX *does not answer*) And with *nothing hanging* out except a protective towel over the back of his sensitive, allergic neck? Now, I ask you, sir, is this the same Dennis Corcoran to whom you attribute nuding about, sitting nude in a rowboat, and thrashing about in nude sex play in the fish pond at your house on that "sunny Sunday"? Is it? I want an answer!

BENDIX (*Finally*)   It is.

SLOANE   Tell me, sir, are you immune to the glandular endowments of young women?

BENDIX   Not any more so or less so than any other healthy man.

SLOANE   The day you testified about—when you claim that Dennis Corcoran came to your house with a certain young woman in . . . a brief bathing suit which made no secret of her glandular endowments . . . Were there any feelings aroused in you by seeing that young, fleshly, well-endowed woman?

BENDIX   Only revulsion.

SLOANE   Not jealousy?

BENDIX   Revulsion.

SLOANE   Not desire?

BENDIX   Revulsion!

SLOANE   Not even a stirring in the loins?

BENDIX   Revulsion!

SLOANE   You stood there and watched and felt none of these things?

BENDIX   None.

SLOANE   How long did you watch?

BENDIX   A time . . .

SLOANE   Hours?

BENDIX   Of course not.

SLOANE   But long enough so you could later give a full and accurate description.

BENDIX   Long enough.

SLOANE   And your wife watched with you?

BENDIX   She has so testified!

SLOANE   And so you expect me—us—to believe that this frail, sensitive, tremulous woman we saw here this morning *chose* to watch the act you so fully described to us?

BENDIX   I don't expect *you* to believe anything!

99

SLOANE I'll tell you what I would believe! (*He moves in close on* BENDIX) I would believe that if such a scene ever did happen, the woman we saw here this morning would have turned her wheelchair about and left that place! I would believe that that scene never *did* happen, except in your filthy imagination!

CLEARY (*Overlapping with above*) Your Honor, I object . . .

BENDIX And I object to this . . . this man . . . standing so close to me!

JUDGE Mr. Sloane, you will confine yourself to questions, not statements. And would you mind standing off a bit from the witness?

SLOANE I'm sorry, Your Honor, but in the heat of battle . . . of course I will stand off. (*He moves to the far wall of the proscenium arch, looks to the* JUDGE *for approval, then starts anew*) Tell me, sir, have you ever heard the phrase "to be Bendixed"?

BENDIX It was created by *Time* magazine and used quite extensively thereafter.

SLOANE Would you say that a fair definition of that word is, to be subjected to the rapier-sharp barbs of criticism created in the distinctive style of Boyd Bendix?

BENDIX It is not my definition, but I would not quarrel with it.

SLOANE Does that style come naturally, easily, or does it take considerable thought and work? For example, when you wrote about Dennis Corcoran, "this hulky, bulky chunk of Irish blubber"—Was that the first phrase that came to your mind? Or did it take a bit of polishing to achieve that rhythm?

BENDIX   One chooses words, changes some, till one finds the proper and most expressive phrase.

SLOANE   And this phrase, also about Dennis Corcoran, "having nothing but gas where a man should have guts." Do those phrases flow trippingly from the pen, as Shakespeare might have said, or are they carefully thought out, polished, the best of a number of alternatives, the rest of which are then discarded as unworthy of the pen of Bendix?

BENDIX   Frankly, Mr. Sloane, you disappoint me. You think you can seduce me through vanity into saying that what I write I write easily and without sweat. You hoped to prove that these statements about Dennis Corcoran were produced carelessly, for carelessness about another man's reputation amounts to malice and malice is an important factor in a case of this kind, isn't it? Well, sir, these words were *not* produced easily, or trippingly, but took belief, honest conviction, hard work, hard concentrated work.

SLOANE   Mr. Bendix, outside of law school that is the most helpful lesson in law I've ever received. And I thank you. Now, I ask you, sir, have you ever heard, or seen, or used the phrase . . . "a three-piece set"?

BENDIX   It . . . it is not familiar to me.

SLOANE Can you guess what it might mean?

BENDIX I haven't the slightest idea of what it means.

SLOANE Might it be one of several phrases you considered while searching for the apt, colorful, memorable phrase, with just the right vigor and style to be remembered by a jury in describing certain parts of a man's anatomy!

BENDIX It is not!

SLOANE Did you not jot it down on a piece of yellow legal paper along with other, alternate phrases, one of which was "lavaliere"?

BENDIX That is a lie!

SLOANE (*As prearranged, he reaches and* DAVID *hands him a straightened but one-time badly rumpled yellow sheet*) And I suggest to *you*, sir, that your memory may be playing tricks on you. That you *did* write down a number of such alternative phrases or words and that one of them was the phrase you actually used on the stand, "lavaliere." Now, think, sir. (*He handles the yellow sheet ever so subtly, yet with enough threat*) Well?

BENDIX I . . . I may have made some notes . . .

SLOANE And I also suggest that the word "lavaliere" was never the word used by a woman like Mrs. Andrews.

BENDIX She did use it!

SLOANE If it was actually the word she used, would you have forgotten it?

BENDIX   As I testified, I did not forget it.

SLOANE   Then why this need for alternatives? Why?

BENDIX   I . . . I was merely . . . scribbling . . . doodling . . . I might have written them down then!

SLOANE   Do you *always* doodle in sexual phrases and images, sir?

CLEARY (*Rising*)   Your Honor, I demand to see that paper!

BENDIX   Paul! No!
        (SLOANE *looks from* CLEARY *to* BENDIX *and back to* CLEARY, *who is powerless now*)

SLOANE   I think we will spare the jury the details of these . . . doodles . . . (*He is relieved to rip up the blank sheet and pour the pieces in* DAVID's *cupped hands. Then he takes up a sheaf of clippings*) Now, sir, I hold here in my hand clippings from such publications as *The Word* . . . *The Puritan* . . . *The Voice of Freedom* . . . *The American Voice* . . . *The Baptist Call* . . . and many, many others . . . all of which you have referred to. All of them remark on the plaintiff in this case, Dennis Corcoran, all of them do so unfavorably.

BENDIX   True.

SLOANE   Are you asking us to believe that you were willing to take the words and opinions of obscure lunatic-fringe publications like these (*Showing the clippings*) as the basis for your evaluation of a man who had been a friend of yours for years?

BENDIX   I call your attention, sir, to the fact that one so-called obscure "lunatic-fringe" publication, like *The Baptist Call*, of which you have never heard, has a larger circulation than the *Atlantic Monthly*, *Harper's* magazine and the *Nation* combined. Three magazines so highly respected by you and your ilk. (*The phrase "you and your ilk" interrupts* SLOANE, *who was reaching to get an exhibit. He turns to face* BENDIX, *who is expectant, almost smiling*) The memories of some are short, Mr. Sloane, but not mine.

SLOANE   What did you mean by "my ilk"?

BENDIX   A certain type of self-appointed, self-ordained "liberal" whose loyalty to the principles of these United States might be questioned.

SLOANE   Are you questioning my loyalty to my country, sir?

BENDIX   I will leave that to the jury! It is not *I* who has brought *that* man into this courtroom, day after day. (*He is indicating* COLES) A hostile witness before Congressional committees, a man forced to resign from the service of our Government! An admitted friend of homosexuals. A man confined in a mental institution for four years! He is *your* friend, *your* associate, not mine! Huddling there with you, whispering, conspiring, plotting how to throttle me. Well, it shall not remain secret much longer. Read my column tomorrow . . . Mr. Abner Coles!

(COLES *rises to protest, but can only stammer*)

COLES   You bastard . . . you unprincipled, outrageous bastard.

(*He begins to tremble uncontrollably*)

JUDGE   Gentlemen! Gentlemen . . .

SLOANE   Ab! Ab . . .
(*He puts his hands gently on* COLES' *shoulders and forces him down into his seat.* DENNIS *and* ANITA *move to help*)

JUDGE   Mr. Sloane, if you wish a recess . . .

SLOANE   Ab? (COLES *shakes his head, negatively; he is regaining control*) Your Honor, we have only one wish. That this trial continue. That it continue *now!* (*During the next few questions* SLOANE *keeps his hands pressed into* COLES' *shoulders till he feels that* COLES *is quite all right*) Mr. Bendix, a moment ago you made certain statements reflecting on my loyalty to my country . . . I would like to know how you arrived at that conclusion.

JUDGE   Surely, Mr. Sloane, you do not intend to engage in an expedition into political philosophy and personal opinion in the midst of this trial?

SLOANE   Sir, we are dealing here *with* opinions! Opinions which verge on calling my client a traitor. Now he has added my associate and myself to his list of victims, because we dare to represent my client. Well, if we are all to be *judged* by Mr. Bendix's opinions, *I* wish to know how he *arrives* at them. And I *will* know before this trial is over!

CLEARY   I object to this whole line of questioning *and* to Mr. Sloane's attitude toward this court!

JUDGE Mr. Cleary, you may assume that this court can protect itself. Mr. Sloane raises a sound question. We *are* dealing with Mr. Bendix's opinions. I will allow it.

SLOANE Now, sir, as to the nature of the Communist conspiracy. Can you describe it for us . . .

BENDIX (*He starts reluctantly but warms up to it*) Through a clever strategy devised in Moscow, the intellectuals of this country have been infiltrated and seduced to the cause of Marxism in the fraudulent guise of social progress. They have allowed themselves and their talents and resources to be subverted and used to spread Communism in the name of Americanism. This disease has infiltrated our schools and colleges, our legislative halls, our churches! Even the Supreme Court and the White House.

SLOANE And the evidences of this infiltration of the intellectuals?

BENDIX Are all about us!

SLOANE For those of us who do not recognize them, would you identify some.

BENDIX Constant agitation! Unrest!

SLOANE Tell me, do you feel that *all* intellectuals are Communists?

BENDIX Of course not all.

SLOANE Most?

BENDIX Many!

106

SLOANE   Now, among the intellectuals you mentioned, how do you tell the "many" from the "most"?

BENDIX   There are signs! Standard Communist causes!

SLOANE   Such as?

BENDIX   They change with the times. They condition the intellectual like Pavlov's dogs, to react to certain words. "Sacco and Vanzetti," "the Scottsboro boys," "fallout." Then they use the magic word and the intellectuals begin signing petitions, joining, carrying placards, marching! We have seen it for fifty years now! Back during the war it was the second front!
   (*This last directed at* DENNIS)

SLOANE   Do you mean that everyone who was for Sacco and Vanzetti was a Communist?

BENDIX   Not everyone.

SLOANE   Everyone who was for the Scottsboro boys was a Communist?

BENDIX   Of course not.

SLOANE   Or everyone who favors equal rights, social and political, for the Negro is a Communist?

BENDIX   No.

SLOANE   Or everyone who would ban the hydrogen bomb?

BENDIX   No!

SLOANE   Then on any scientific or logical basis these are *not* tests for Communists, are they?

107

BENDIX   Your Honor, he is harassing me again! I want him to stand away from me.

JUDGE (*Gaveling the dispute to silence*)   Mr. Sloane, is it necessary to stand quite that close?

SLOANE   To Mr. Bendix or to *you*, sir?

JUDGE   Please, Mr. Sloane . . .

SLOANE (*Lightly*)   After Mr. Bendix's vague and mysterious description of the symptomatology of Communism I wouldn't blame Your Honor for suspecting that it was a sub-microscopic virus transmitted secretly from victim to victim. That was all I meant, sir.

JUDGE   Mr. Sloane, you will continue with your examination, saving any comments for your summation.

SLOANE (*To* BENDIX)   Tell me, sir, how long have you studied the phenomenon of Communism?

BENDIX   More than twenty years.

SLOANE   Would you consider yourself an expert in the field?

BENDIX   I would.

SLOANE   And being an expert, once you arrived at the determination that my client, Dennis Corcoran, was a Red then you wrote the following aimed at getting him fired from his magazine . . . "any advertiser or magazine who carries the words of this Commie-oriented blabbermouth should consider carefully the effect on its readers . . ."

CLEARY   Objection! There is no testimony whatsoever that Mr. Corcoran's firing resulted in any way from Mr. Bendix's columns!

SLOANE (*In full memory of* ALSTON)   No, there isn't, is there, Mr. Cleary?

CLEARY (*Just as aware of* ALSTON)   I'm sure, Mr. Sloane, that if this were true and there were any witnesses to the fact, you would have brought them into this courtroom long before this.

SLOANE   Mr. Bendix, you testified you considered it your duty to warn the American public about Mr. Corcoran's Red tendencies. Just how did you arrive at that determination?

BENDIX   It was based on what he said, what he wrote, what he did. He went to Moscow during the war.

SLOANE   As a Red, or as a war correspondent?

BENDIX   I'm afraid *he* can answer that better than I can!

SLOANE   Tell me, did you think that Corcoran was a Red when you first met him?

BENDIX   No.

SLOANE   Do you have any idea when he began to change? Was it a sudden change, or gradual . . .

BENDIX   Such changes are usually slow . . .

SLOANE   If I read to you from the writings of the man could you tell, by applying your expertise, whether or not he had yet come under the Communist influence . . .

BENDIX I could.

SLOANE *(Turning to* COLES, *who hands him a long memo of some pages)* I quote now, this statement from the writings of Dennis Corcoran . . . "There is a move away from anything old, since to most of the world's people the old is what they have had and hate and suspect. Hence they feel the new cannot be as bad as the old." Your opinion of that statement, sir?

BENDIX The choice of words, the flavor, the texture of the statement itself show clearly that it was Moscow-inspired.

SLOANE This texture, this flavor, this color, is there a litmus paper test for it? Or is this talent for detecting colors exclusive to you?

BENDIX You study the Communist conspiracy, you discern a technique, you analyze it and thus become an expert at it.

SLOANE And, of course, once you see it, it is your duty to let other Americans know?

BENDIX It is.

SLOANE I read now from another Corcoran article which goes as follows: "Whatever our differences with the Communists they are our allies and I can tell you this, from first-hand experience under fire on both sides of the continent, the color of blood is red, theirs and ours." Would you analyze that statement for us?

BENDIX Oh, that one, yes: He was deep in by that time. Forget differences. Make a common front. The striking image of blood being a bond between the peoples and blood being red . . . it all adds up to "let's be friends with the Communists."

SLOANE He didn't say friends, he said allies, which was a fact at the time, wasn't it?

BENDIX Some people knew better. Churchill said it, straight out. The day when Russia was invaded by the Nazis. "I would fight on the side of the devil if the devil were fighting Hitler!"

SLOANE The same Winston Churchill whose letter of commendation to Dennis Corcoran was read in this courtroom on a previous day?

BENDIX The same man, and now that you mention it, with the same motives as well. Just as Churchill would greet Stalin as an ally if he were fighting Hitler so he could commend Corcoran, no matter *what* he stood for, as long as he was helping England win the war!

　　(BENDIX *quite obviously thinks he's scored a point.* SLOANE *is fattening him up and throwing him off guard*)

SLOANE (*Smiles, shrugs, as though trapped and acknowledging it. Meantime he switches the quote sheets with* COLES) I deserve that, sir. Nothing is more comical in cross-examination, or in fishing, than to see the fisherman pulled into the water by his catch. Now, another statement if you will. I quote . . . (*He is reading from the new set of quotes*) "Poverty, exploitation, utter lack of hope, are the foods on which Communism feeds . . . The best breeding ground for Communism is the empty belly. Men will grasp at any philosophy or movement that promises food to their children."

BENDIX   Ah, doesn't *that* have a familiar ring!

SLOANE   Communist?

BENDIX   Communist.

SLOANE   Now, this statement, sir: "Instead of blaming Communism, let us blame ourselves. The sick man will seek out any doctor, even a witch doctor. We can't blame him. *He* has the pain in his belly, not *we*." Would you characterize the man who wrote that statement?

BENDIX   Communist-leaning, party-lining lout.

SLOANE   Communist-leaning, party-lining lout.

BENDIX   Don't you see through it? Setting up the world as being sick and Communism as being the only doctor for that sickness!

SLOANE   But the phrase "witch doctor"—doesn't that *disparage* Communism rather than praise it?

BENDIX   Exactly! That's the tip-off!

SLOANE   What is?

BENDIX   The seeming use of a disparaging phrase in order to throw off the unsuspecting. An innocent reader seeing that statement in a magazine article would say to himself, If Corcoran *were* a Red would he use a phrase like "witch doctor" about Communism?

SLOANE   I see. So that by *disparaging* Communism a man would actually be a better Communist than by *praising* it?

BENDIX   In certain circumstances.

SLOANE   Then you would say that the man who wrote this is not only Communist, or Communist-inclined, but very skillful at it?

BENDIX   I would. And I would feel compelled to expose him. And I did!

SLOANE   Who, sir?

BENDIX   Dennis Corcoran!

SLOANE   *I* was talking about the man who wrote *these* Communist-inspired, *leftist* statements.

BENDIX   And so am I!

SLOANE   They are not the same man . . .

BENDIX   But you read . . .

SLOANE   Certain statements by Dennis Corcoran. (SLOANE *points to* COLES, *who holds up the Corcoran quotes*) Then certain *other* statements . . . the last few (SLOANE *brandishes the pages he holds*) by *another* well-known writer of our time. A man whom you have just characterized as being Communist . . . in fact, if I remember correctly that immortal phrase . . . "A Communist-leaning, party-lining lout." (*Turning to the* JUDGE) Your Honor, I would like to offer in evidence this sheet containing certain writings from the columns of one Boyd Bendix!

BENDIX   That's a lie! A fraud!

SLOANE   Here are the excerpts. Here are photostats of the original columns as they appeared! Examine them first, then cry "fraud"! (*He shoves them at* BENDIX) Are those true and correct excerpts from these columns of yours? (*When* BENDIX *does not answer*) Your Honor, I demand that the witness be directed to answer that question!

JUDGE   Mr. Bendix?

BENDIX   I will not answer any question till this man stands off there.

JUDGE   Mr. Bendix, you will answer the question put to you!

BENDIX (*Holding up the fistful of clippings*)   Yes, I will answer the question! Lie, fraud! Trick! Cheap, underhanded trick! They couldn't attack Bendix any other way, couldn't smear him or dirty him, because his life is clean, his motives are clean! So they sent for this . . . this man . . . who is known for his snide, clever, underhanded, crafty methods in the courtroom and they said, "Get Bendix! Any way you can! Any way you can!" And what did he do? He culled carefully through Bendix's writings over the years and out of millions of words took a few phrases out of context, read them with a kind of accent and emphasis that deliberately made them sound like Corcoran's writings! Did he say straight out and forthright, "Here is Corcoran, here is Bendix, analyze them both"? An honest man puts honest questions. He does not come with *parts* of questions, with veiled words, or hidden sources! I know you now. Your guile is the guile of Sloane, but your evil is the evil of Moscow. I will unmask you for what you are! And I will destroy you!

CLEARY   Your Honor, my client is under great emotional strain . . . I ask that this entire statement be stricken from the record!

SLOANE   Your Honor, the witness has been responsive to my questions. He has shown us and the jury the Bendix reflex in action, and what a malicious thing it is. I insist that his answer remain in the record.

BENDIX   You took my words out of context! Here! Read them *all*!

SLOANE   I *have* read them all. And evidently more recently than you have. And *I know* it is unfair to show half a man's face and ask, what does he *look* like? Or half his brain and ask, what does he *think* like? But that's exactly what you did in your vicious effort to assassinate Dennis Corcoran! (*He moves away from* BENDIX, *slowly, deliberately, then turns to look at him*) Now, I'm afraid, sir, that *you* have been standing too close to *me*. And frankly, I don't like it.
    (*There is a moment of silence and* BENDIX *sinks down into the witness chair for the first time*)

Blackout

SCENE 2

Several days later. The lights come up slowly. CLEARY *has been speaking in summation.* BENDIX's *chair is empty.*

CLEARY ". . . this baboon who walks like a man would surrender us to the forces of racial degradation." And these words, ladies and gentlemen . . . "I have seen ring-tailed monkeys hanging from trees, who had greater understanding and respect for this country and its problems. This ugly, awkward, deceitful, grotesque fool is a traitor to this nation and what it stands for." Those, ladies and gentlemen, are words written and printed in the public press about one Abraham Lincoln. Did he sue? Did he go running to the courts to cry "help"? No. For he knew, as does every man in public life, that when you enter that arena you subject yourself to the view and the criticism of all people. President Truman said it another way. "If you can't stand the heat stay out of the kitchen." It's an old American custom. Now surely a newspaperman like Dennis Corcoran knows that! Then why is he here? Because he lives on conflict, his reputation was made in a war. But there has been no war recently. And the name of Dennis Corcoran is heard less and less. So, stir up the world, come into court, make a private war! Yet, if there was substance to this lawsuit, they should be able to prove damage, serious damage. But aside from a piddling matter of one speech that was canceled, we heard no witness say, "Bendix deprived Corcoran of his livelihood."

We heard no one testify, "He was fired because of what Bendix wrote." But I will go a step further. Even if we had before us proof, indisputable proof that Corcoran suffered a loss of income, that would still not make us liable. Because as a newspaperman Boyd Bendix had every right to make fair comment about Dennis Corcoran. And even Corcoran's distinguished lawyer will not deny that. He can't. Because it is in our Constitution, big as life, clear as day. *Not* Congress, *not* the states, *not any one* shall make a law abridging freedom of the press. Surely then, not a jury. No, I say, Dennis Corcoran started this fight, provoked this whole controversy by attacking my client in print. And you, the jury, should say to him now, "This is a backyard scrap between friends. Break it up and go home. And next time, pick on a fellow your own size, mentally." Bendix is no Goliath, Corcoran no David.

(CLEARY *sits down*)

JUDGE   Mr. Sloane.

(SLOANE *rises, to face the jury*)

SLOANE   May it please the court, ladies and gentlemen of the jury . . . Something is different in this courtroom. A chair that was occupied every day since this trial began is empty today . . . (*He turns to* BENDIX's *chair*) Perhaps to give some visual support to Mr. Cleary's argument that nothing of importance is going on here. "Just a backyard scrap between two friends." Well, I say it moved out of the category of a scrap between two friends when this man decided to call my client vicious names in the full sight of fourteen million people every day. For those charges, sexual and political, were made with a professional skill that one does not find in backyards or over fences. And made in such colorful, polished, suggestive language that you would not forget them. Language that he worked at diligently, as you will recall. Now, the charge of Communism is the more serious one. Because the threat of Communism is serious. In a free society we must ever be alert to *all* who would destroy us, Fascist or Communist, right or left. But they must be identified with precision, with responsibility, not out of malicious personal vindictiveness. For the loose or capricious accusation does more to *destroy* our freedom than to *protect* it. (*Speaking to the chair*) You, who judge and condemn others at your whim, where are you when your conduct is being judged? Hiding? Like a malicious little boy who has written dirty words on a wall and then run away to let someone else wipe the words off! Words scribbled there large enough for fourteen million people to see—"coward . . . pervert . . . sex fiend . . . liar . . . Red . . . Communist . . ." All unproved, untrue. And now he leaves Mr. Cleary to try to wash them off. But Mr. Cleary couldn't, so he tried to cover them up. With the flag. With the holy words "Constitution," "Freedom of the Press." Now I do not scoff at these words. Particularly not at Freedom of the Press. Because it was made good with the blood of human beings in those times when the Press was one little man and a hand press, who dared to speak out against the King. The Press *needed* protection, if freedom were ever to prevail. But today the Press is multimillion-dollar organizations, with millions of readers. Strong enough to criticize the Government and its officials loudly, openly, freely, without fear of reprisal. (*He turns to the chair*) Sir, let me ask you, when you express *your* opinions do you take your life in your hands? Have *you* ever been threatened? *Have* you? (*He takes a pause*) If he were here, he could not say "yes." Because he *has* Freedom of the Press. But who protects Dennis Corcoran who has been called vile and untrue names? *You do!* For the law places it in your hands to decide if the Constitution intends that Bendix has the right, unrestricted, unlimited, to destroy the lives and careers of other people with lies. And then to wrap himself in the flag and Constitution and cry out, "Touch me not lest you destroy Freedom of the Press." No, I think we would be doing more here for Freedom of the Press if you said to Bendix, and to News International, "Dennis Corcoran has been Bendixed and we will not stand for it." Because freedom is for everybody or nobody! Because every man is entitled to hold an opinion and voice it. Or soon nobody is. Because you cannot intimidate one man without making all men a little bit afraid. Now, *how* do you *repay* Corcoran for the damage that has been done to him? Especially since that damage will not be finished when we walk out of this courtroom. For years after this trial is over, whenever the name Dennis Corcoran comes up for an assignment, at a big magazine or a radio and television network, the places where correspondents and commentators are hired, *or* fired, someone will say, "Wasn't he in some kind of trouble? Who needs trouble?" They will forget that "the trouble" he was in consisted of being accused by *one* man who lied about him. How do you pay a man for jobs as yet unlost? For doors so silently closed in his face that he never even knows when it happens? For the cowardice and prejudice of other people who say, "who needs trouble"? Well, the law provides a way. Punitive damages. To be awarded when the jury feels the defendants have acted recklessly, maliciously. Remember, that unless your verdict is high enough, costly enough to this multimillion-dollar corporation and to this absent, arrogant defendant, you will be giving them a license to go out and do this all over again to some other poor victim! Unless you do this, you have opened the door to a reign of terror-by-accusation, destruction-by-falsehood, murder-by-suspicion. We are in a civil court. But *crimes* are being judged here! The worst crimes of our age. By your verdict it will be determined if these crimes will be allowed to go unpunished.

(*He turns away toward the table as the lights go down*)

Blackout

John Randolph, Joel Crothers, Van Heflin, M'el Dowd,
and Joseph Julian, as DENNIS CORCORAN, DAVID STRONG,
ROBERT SLOANE, ANITA CORCORAN, and ABNER COLES

It is twelve hours later. The lights come up dimly on the courtroom, where all the participants except BENDIX *wait for the verdict.* DENNIS, *naturally more nervous than all the others, is reaching for another cigarette.*

DENNIS I'm going out to grab another smoke.

SLOANE If anything happens, we'll call you.
(DENNIS *exits.* ANITA *rises intending to go after him but there is nothing she can do to comfort him.* SLOANE *reaches out to clasp her hand and comfort her. They are interrupted by the entry of the* CLERK. *He moves quickly, and with purpose, up to the door to the judge's chambers. All come alert at this hint of a verdict. The* CLERK *turns from the door to announce*)

CLERK All rise!
(SLOANE *signals* DAVID *to get* DENNIS. *Meantime, the* JUDGE *enters pulling on his robe. The jury* FORE-MAN *enters. As the* JUDGE *ascends the bench*)

JUDGE I have been informed that the ladies and gentlemen of the jury have finally reached a verdict.

FOREMAN We have, Your Honor.

JUDGE What is that verdict?

FOREMAN We find for the plaintiff Dennis Corcoran compensatory damages in the sum of one dollar.

DAVID (*Half rising*)   No!
(COLES *forces him down*)

JUDGE (*To the* FOREMAN)   Continue.

FOREMAN   We also find for the plaintiff punitive damages in the sum of five hundred thousand dollars against Defendant News International. And one hundred thousand dollars against Defendant Boyd Bendix.
(*The first stir of jubilation is held in check till the* JUDGE *says*)

JUDGE   Thank you, ladies and gentlemen of the jury. This trial stands adjourned!
(*Now the jubilation, led by* DAVID, *explodes.* DAVID *and* COLES *are up and pounding* DENNIS *on the back.* SLOANE *to* ANITA)

SLOANE   What do you think of our courts and our justice now?
(*She kisses* SLOANE *on the cheek.* DENNIS *grasps his hand*)

DENNIS   One thing, Bob . . . that first day . . . those things I said about you . . . will you forgive me?

SLOANE   I will not! That's what every lawyer needs, somebody to shake him up periodically and remind him why he went to law school in the first place. Now, you two go on home and get some sleep. We'll celebrate tomorrow.
(DENNIS *and* ANITA *exit.* CLEARY *comes across, carrying hat and briefcase. He passes* SLOANE *without a word*)
Paul . . .

(*As* CLEARY *turns back,* SLOANE *gives him Church-ill's V-for-victory sign.* CLEARY *exits.* COLES *comes down to shake* SLOANE'*s hand*)

COLES   Bob, when you win one like this, you win it for everybody.

SLOANE   If winning were the end of it. But this fight has to be fought and won over and over. In our time, in *his* time (*Indicating* DAVID), in every time.
(COLES *exits to get* SLOANE'*s hat and coat, leaving* SLOANE *and* DAVID *alone*)

DAVID   Sir, it was a privilege to be here, to watch and learn.

SLOANE   And did you? Learn, I mean.

DAVID   Yes, sir!

SLOANE   Good! Because every law firm needs at least one junior partner who can read upside down.

Curtain

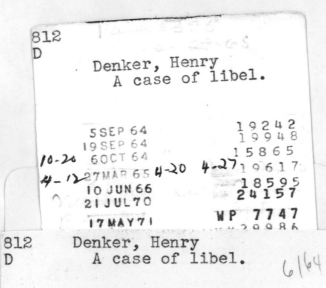

812
D

Denker, Henry
A case of libel.

5 SEP 64	1 9 2 4 2
19 SEP 64	1 9 9 4 8
10-20 6 OCT 64	1 5 8 6 5
4-12 27 MAR 65 4-20 4-27	9 6 1 7
10 JUN 66	1 8 5 9 5
21 JUL 70	2 4 1 5 7
17 MAY 71	W P 7 7 4 7

812
D

Denker, Henry
A case of libel.

6/64